W9-DEL-629

# DATE DUE
# REMINDER

## Please do not remove
## this date due slip.

*Dancock's Dance*

One of Canada's most acclaimed writers, Guy Vanderhaeghe is the author of three collections of short stories, two novels, and two plays. His short story collection *Man Descending* won the Governor General's Award for fiction and the Geoffrey Faber Memorial Prize in Great Britain. His novel *Homesick* was a co-winner of the City of Toronto Book Award. Mr Vanderhaeghe's fiction has been translated and published in seven languages. His play, *I Had A Job I Liked. Once.* was first produced at the Persephone Theatre and went on to win the Canadian Authors Association prize for the best drama. *Dancock's Dance* had its debut production at the Persephone Theatre in 1995.

# Dancock's Dance

by Guy Vanderhaeghe

**Blizzard Publishing** • Winnipeg

*Dancock's Dance* first published 1996 by
Blizzard Publishing Inc.
73 Furby Street, Winnipeg, Canada R3C 2A2
© 1996 Guy Vanderhaeghe

Cover art by Robert Pasternak.
Printed in Canada by Friesens Printing Ltd.

Published with the assistance of
the Canada Council and the Manitoba Arts Council.

### Caution

Canadian Cataloguing in Publication Data

Vanderhaeghe, Guy, 1951–
  Dancock's dance
  A play.
  ISBN 0-921368-61-5
I. Title.
PS8593.A5386D35 1996   C812'.54   C95-920256-0
PR9199.3.V384D35 1996

To Margaret, who never gave up on *Dancock's Dance* and wouldn't let me either.
And to the director and cast, who finally brought it to life.

*Dancock's Dance* was first performed at the Persephone Theatre, Saskatoon, Saskatchewan, on April 1, 1995, with the following cast:

| | |
|---|---|
| DANCOCK | Joel Kaiser |
| The SOLDIER | Hume Baugh |
| The SUPERINTENDENT | Paul Rainville |
| BRAUN | Tibor Feheregyhazi |
| KENNEALY | Rob Roy |
| DOROTHEA | Marina Stephenson Kerr |

Directed by Bill Glasco
Set and costume design by David Skelton
Lighting design by Allan Stichbury
Stage Manager: Laura Kennedy

## Characters

DANCOCK: Lieutenant John Carlyle Dancock, patient and former officer, age 25 to 35.

The SOLDIER: A figure from Dancock's past, age 25 to 35.

The SUPERINTENDENT: Administrator and chief medical officer of the Saskatchewan Hospital for the Insane, late middle-age.

BRAUN: Rudy Braun, patient and German immigrant, middle-aged.

KENNEALY: Kevin Kennealy, orderly in the hospital.

DOROTHEA: Dorothea Gage, voluntary patient, age 21 to 30.

## Setting

The main action of the play takes place in the Saskatchewan Hospital for the Insane, North Battleford, Saskatchewan, during the late fall of 1918 as World War I concludes and the Spanish influenza epidemic breaks out.

# Act One

## Scene One

*(The stage is dark except for LIEUTENANT JOHN CARLYLE DANCOCK seated on his bed in the Saskatchewan Hospital for the Insane. His suit is the height of fashion for gentlemen in the year 1918. The SOLDIER enters. To the audience he is only a shadow, a dim figure hovering at Dancock's back. DANCOCK, sensing something, a disconcerting presence, grows uneasy. A popular tune from the First World War starts to softly play and the shadowy SOLDIER begins to dance to it. The dance is unsettling, a hint of subtle menace contained in it. DANCOCK scratches the backs of his hands, his agitation and desperation mounting as the dance carries on behind him. The SOLDIER exits, the music dies. DANCOCK lifts his hands, looks at them.)*

## Scene Two

*(Two figures are lit on a dark stage. DANCOCK seated on his bed, staring down at his hands resting on his knees. The SUPERINTENDENT, standing to one side, studying him with compassion. The SUPERINTENDENT is a man in late middle-age, tweedy, a blend of "progressive" doctor and scientific authoritarian. He addresses the audience in a strong, quiet, clinical manner. As he talks, the lights imperceptibly edge up until when he finishes speaking the stage is washed in late afternoon sunlight.)*

SUPERINTENDENT: *(Indicating DANCOCK.)* Lieutenant John Carlyle Dancock, formerly of the 5th Battalion, Western Cavalry. Twice decorated for conspicuous bravery, twice wounded. January of 1918 invalided back to Canada, judged unfit for further service. Diagnosis, acute neurasthenia. In layman's language—severe shellshock. Condition worsened in months following his demobilization. March of 1918, shouted down a sermon urging patriotic sacrifice and was arrested for disrupting a church service. Because of war record released with a warning. *(Pause.)* Returned the next Sunday and poured blood in the collection plate. Brought before a provincial magistrate and judged insane under the provisions of the Insanity Act of 1906. Committed to the Saskatchewan Hospital for the Insane, April 12, 1918. *(Pause.)* A man of good family, educated, obviously intelligent ... sensitive. While not as profoundly ill as many patients, demonstrates symptoms of hysteria and melancholia. Exhibits fixed paranoid mania in regard to persons of authority. To date, uncooperative and hostile to treatment. A difficult case. A difficult patient. *(Pause.)* I do what I can.

*(The SUPERINTENDENT enters DANCOCK's ward, walks to the edge of his bed, looks hard at DANCOCK's hands. )*

You felt uneasy again today.

*(The SUPERINTENDENT points to DANCOCK's hands. DANCOCK hides them in his jacket pockets.)*

I'll have matron bring you some salve from the Infirmary. A little ointment will do wonders.

*(DANCOCK remains silent. The SUPERINTENDENT continues casually.)*

Fine weather today. Sky as blue as a Dutchman's britches. But you, according to Mr. Kennealy, preferred to sit on your bed rather than join the other men and help with the threshing. (Pause.) Refusing once again to help yourself.

*(DANCOCK remains silent.)*

You know my views. Hard work in the open air is therapeutic.

DANCOCK: Hard work without pay is slavery.

SUPERINTENDENT: The other men would not agree with you. They were happy to be free in the sun and fresh air. None of them would have changed places with you.

DANCOCK: None of them are in their right minds. Presumably, that is the reason they find themselves here.

SUPERINTENDENT: Your friend Braun enjoyed it well enough.

*(DANCOCK says nothing. )*

Your friendship with him—I find it curious.

DANCOCK: Why?

SUPERINTENDENT: He is a German.

DANCOCK: *(Correcting him.)* An immigrant from Germany.

SUPERINTENDENT: And you spent the last three years killing Germans and watching your comrades be killed by Germans.

DANCOCK: Correct.

SUPERINTENDENT: Yet you befriend one.

DANCOCK: The German soldier did his duty. I did mine. He was an honest enemy. *(Pause.)* I save my hatred for dishonest enemies. The ones who pretend to be your friend, then stab you in the back.

SUPERINTENDENT: Ah, yes. Manufacturers who shipped you rifles that jammed and lined their pockets with the profits. Politicians who promised the war would be over by Christmas, year after year after year. Teachers, clergymen ... *(Beat.)* You see, I've heard you recite your roll call of scoundrels so often I know it by heart.

DANCOCK: *(Cutting.)* By heart? *(Pause.)* No, not by heart.

*(The SUPERINTENDENT is stung by this retort.)*

SUPERINTENDENT: Have you never asked yourself whether you foster this friendship with Braun because he is weak? Easily led?

*(DANCOCK laughs.)*

You have a talent for leadership, Lieutenant Dancock. It makes you a dangerous influence. On the other patients.

DANCOCK: Me, a leader? That I never was.

SUPERINTENDENT: You were a good soldier once. *(Earnestly.)* Be a good soldier again. Place yourself under orders.

DANCOCK: Whose orders?

SUPERINTENDENT: Mine.

*(DANCOCK laughs.)*

I can help you.

DANCOCK: To hell with your help. I don't want it.

SUPERINTENDENT: Let me relieve your misery. *(With conviction.)* I can help you.

DANCOCK: *(Angrily.)* Help me? Like the magistrate who committed me here? Like the lying politicians? Like the generals?

SUPERINTENDENT: *(With dignity.)* I am a doctor. Not a general.

DANCOCK: The hell you're not! Your only concern is for the big picture, strategy, the theory. And like a general you are deaf and blind to what goes on in the ranks.

SUPERINTENDENT: What is it I don't know?

DANCOCK: I would keep an eye on Orderly Kennealy if I were you.

SUPERINTENDENT: Why? Because he advised me to stop your newspapers?

DANCOCK: Which you did.

SUPERINTENDENT: Mr. Kennealy felt news of the war excited you over much. I happen to agree with him.

DANCOCK: Would it excite you over much if I told you that yesterday Kennealy asked me to give him an old suit of mine?

SUPERINTENDENT: *(Taken aback.)* I don't believe it.

DANCOCK: *(Sardonically.)* My word as an officer and a gentleman.

SUPERINTENDENT: Then I shall have a word with Mr. Kennealy.

DANCOCK: While you're at it, tell him to stop calling me the "Red Bolshevik" behind my back.

SUPERINTENDENT: If you insist on railing against the Government and the war, then you must expect simple men to misunderstand. He would consider it treason to talk as you do.

DANCOCK: And what do you consider it?

SUPERINTENDENT: The conduct of the war does not concern me, my patients do. I have endeavoured to make this hospital an island untouched by war, untouched by the smell of death. When things begin to break apart—nations or men—the cure is not more breaking, more anarchy. The cracked pot is not mended by smashing it to the floor.

DANCOCK: *(Furious.)* What difference does it make? If the pot is a bad pot, smash it! Break it to bits!

SUPERINTENDENT: One of the differences between us, Lieutenant Dancock, is that I do not believe all our misery can be blamed on those in authority. I am rather more old-fashioned and concur with Dr. Johnson: "How small, of all that human hearts endure, / That part which laws or kings can cause or cure!" *(Pause.)* Of course, your opinions are your own. Your conduct, however, is an entirely different matter.

DANCOCK: *(Suspicious.)* My conduct?

SUPERINTENDENT: From the moment you were admitted to this hospital your case has been of great interest to me, Lieutenant Dancock. One naturally feels a special kinship and sympathy with a man of similar education and background.

DANCOCK: *(Sarcastic.)* Does one?

SUPERINTENDENT: But now I see I was wrong to indulge you. I was wrong to grant you special privileges.

DANCOCK: Privileges! What privileges!

SUPERINTENDENT: You refuse to work. You refuse to obey lights out. Henceforward this will stop. You will obey the rules. Without exception. Your disruptions of the good order and discipline of this hospital will no longer be tolerated.

DANCOCK: What disruptions have I created?

SUPERINTENDENT: The incident at last Wednesday's tea dance. It was selfish and irresponsible of you to spoil the occasion for the other patients.

DANCOCK: I spoiled nothing for the other patients.

SUPERINTENDENT: *(Sharply.)* No? And whom did you invite to dance?

DANCOCK: I do not know her name. You rudely interrupted us before introductions were completed.

SUPERINTENDENT: You know it is not permitted for patients to dance with patients. You may dance with a nurse. A female patient may dance with an orderly. But under no circumstances will patients be allowed to dance with patients.

DANCOCK: Why?

SUPERINTENDENT: Do not play the village idiot, Dancock. The reasons are obvious.

DANCOCK: Not to me.

SUPERINTENDENT: *(Losing patience.)* You know as well as I, there are men here who cannot govern their sexual impulses. Who masturbate on the wards, in public!

DANCOCK: Such men are beside the point, Superintendent, they would never be given permission to attend tea dances. And you know it.

SUPERINTENDENT: Scandal of any kind is a threat to the reforms I have instituted here: nourishing food, hydrotherapy—

DANCOCK: Hydrotherapy! You call that a reform? Sitting in a bath of ice water hour after hour? Standing under a needle spray until the Second Coming?

SUPERINTENDENT: All the best authorities recommend hydrotherapy as a sedative.

DANCOCK: And work without pay? Is that a sedative also?

SUPERINTENDENT: Therapeutic work is a reform! As are the weekly tea dances for patients. And I will not put my reforms at risk. If any charge of sexual impropriety were to be made by a patient's family, the Government would jump at the opportunity to turn this place into a prison. It is cheaper to lock people up than to cure them.

DANCOCK: I will dance with whomever I choose.

SUPERINTENDENT: Be careful, Lieutenant, or you may find yourself dancing with the devil.

*(The two men stare challengingly at one another for some time. Finally, the SUPERINTENDENT takes out his pocket watch and consults it. He has made up his mind and there is no going back.)*

Six-thirty. Those who went threshing today will soon be returning to the ward.

DANCOCK: And they'll have had meat for supper because they did your bidding. Carrots for the donkeys.

SUPERINTENDENT: I'll leave you now so you can prepare for bed.

DANCOCK: I am not going to bed. Not even a child goes to bed at seven o'clock with the sun shining in his eyes.

SUPERINTENDENT: Extended rest is a part of the treatment. You will retire at seven o'clock. If you refuse, Mr. Kennealy will see to it you are put to bed. In restraints. Is that understood?

DANCOCK: So the carrot having failed, the donkey is to feel the stick?

SUPERINTENDENT: That is for the donkey to decide.

DANCOCK: Bastard! I despise you and your kind for what you did to me.

SUPERINTENDENT: And what did my kind do to you?

DANCOCK: *(With emotion.)* Changed me. I want to be what I once was.

SUPERINTENDENT: *(Eagerly.)* But if you let me, I can help mend what has been broken in you. I can—

DANCOCK: Not broken! Changed! Changed!

*(The SUPERINTENDENT puts a comforting hand on DANCOCK's shoulder. He violently flings it off and glares up at the SUPERINTENDENT.)*

SUPERINTENDENT: Remember, bed at seven o'clock.

DANCOCK: Go to hell.

*(The SUPERINTENDENT starts for the door, hesitates, turns back.)*

SUPERINTENDENT: Twenty years ago I was a young doctor working in an insane asylum in Ontario. Every day, rain or shine, summer or winter, a poor unfortunate kept his post at the entrance to the asylum. There he accosted all visitors, accusing them of murdering his wife and babies.

*(A pause.)*

DANCOCK: *(Impatiently.)* And?

SUPERINTENDENT: He had murdered them himself.

*(The SUPERINTENDENT exits. His story makes a great impression on DANCOCK. Clearly shaken, he resumes obsessively clawing his hands. RUDOLPH BRAUN, a German immigrant, rushes into the ward puppyishly eager, but the sight of DANCOCK raking his hands with his nails brings him up short. He approaches slowly and carefully, as if stealing up on a skittish animal. He takes DANCOCK's hands and begins to gently and compassionately stroke them with his fingertips.)*

BRAUN: *(With a slight German accent.)* Poor, poor hands. They bleed. Ja? *(Reproachfully.)* Look how you treat them, those hands.

*(DANCOCK seizes BRAUN's hands and prevents him from continuing to stroke him.)*

Seven wagons full of stooks I loaded today. *(Beat.)* Seven times seven wagon loads of stooks I loaded!

DANCOCK: Well done, Rudy.

BRAUN: *(Suddenly ebullient, pointing to DANCOCK's suit.)* I like very much that suit. Did I buy it for you? I have bought many people suits. I see my suits wherever I go. Just this morning I met the good Superintendent in the corridor and he too was wearing the suit I bought for him. I congratulated him upon his good appearance.

DANCOCK: That was generous of you.

BRAUN: I am a generous man. Let me write you a cheque.

> *(BRAUN takes out a scrap of paper and scribbles on it. He presents it to DANCOCK with a flourish.)*

A thousand dollars for you. Any bank will honour my cheque. All the banks know Rudolph Braun. The Bank of Montreal will honour it. The Imperial Bank of Canada. The Bank of Nova Scotia. Even the Bank of England. The Bank of England knows of my connection with the English royal family. The English royal family are Germans like me. Also immigrants. From Hanover they were invited to be kings of the English. From Cologne I was invited to be king of the Canadians.

DANCOCK: And how glad we are you accepted.

BRAUN: I got a good price for my bakery so I came. *(Snaps his fingers.)* Just like that, Mama and Rudy and the little ones came.

> *(KENNEALY, in a white orderly's smock, enters. He observes BRAUN who, unaware of his presence, cheerfully rambles on.)*

The husband of Queen Victoria was also a German. His name was Prince Albert. Queen Victoria required a German for the fulfilling sex act. Germans are champions of the sex act.

DANCOCK: Of course. That is common knowledge.

BRAUN: Nobody but a German could fill her up.

> *(Just then BRAUN spots KENNEALY. He looks about him like a cornered rabbit, panics, throws his arms over his head, scuttles past KENNEALY and out of the ward.)*

KENNEALY: Daft bastard. I'll be glad when this war's over and they can ship him back to Germany as an undesirable alien. Let their Dr. Frankensteins have at him.

DANCOCK: Watch your tongue. He's a friend of mine.

KENNEALY: *(Ingratiatingly.)* Ah well, but you're the lad with a heart of gold. Sympathy for all. Especially the poor working devil like Kennealy who has no choice but to do the bidding of mucky-mucks and uppity-ups.

DANCOCK: Don't try it on with me, Kennealy. I'm not going to bed at seven o'clock.

KENNEALY: Ah, but don't you see? Neither of us has any choice in the matter. His nibs has laid down the law. It's going to be done easy, or done hard. But done. So why don't you be the nice gentleman, put on your nightshirt and save us all some trouble?

DANCOCK: Kiss my arse!

KENNEALY: *(Over his shoulder.)* Mr. Cooper! Mr. Oswald! *(Pause.)* You know me, sir. Live and let live. *(Pause.)* There's still time to change your mind before the gorillas arrive.

DANCOCK: Change your own mind.

KENNEALY: Ah well, it's not my mind to change, is it? It's the Super's.

*(They wait. Outside, the sound of orderlies approaching.)*

### Scene Three

*(The lights slowly come up until DANCOCK is just visible in his bed. The SOLDIER enters and halts a few feet inside the entrance, a dim figure loitering. DANCOCK, sensing his presence, stirs, tries to sit up but cannot. He is strapped down.)*

DANCOCK: Is that you, Kennealy? *(Pause.)* Come on then, unstrap me. *(Pause.)* The point's been made. Let me loose. *(Pause.)* What's your game, Kennealy? Answer me, you bastard!

*(DANCOCK struggles furiously in his bonds. The SOLDIER watches, motionless. DANCOCK, exhausted, gives up.)*

What do you want, Kennealy? *(Pause.)* What do you want, you arse-licking counter jumper?

SOLDIER: You've been disobedient. They make you pay a price. *(Pause.)* I did.

DANCOCK: *(Uncertain.)* Kennealy?

SOLDIER: Not Kennealy.

DANCOCK: Who then?

SOLDIER: *(Moving towards the bed.)* A lad.

DANCOCK: A lad? What lad?

SOLDIER: Just a lad.

DANCOCK: *(Alarmed.)* A patient? How did you get off your ward?

SOLDIER: Not a patient.

DANCOCK: Who then? What business have you with me?

SOLDIER: Business? I've come to invite you to the dance.

DANCOCK: What dance? You mean the Superintendent's bloody tea dance?

SOLDIER: No. The one you sent me to.

DANCOCK: What's this nonsense you're talking? I never sent anyone to a dance.

SOLDIER: It's wrong to send another, sir. And not go yourself.

DANCOCK: *(A suspicion dawning on him.)* Who are you? Come closer.

> *(The SOLDIER steps nearer the bed.)*

Closer! I can't make out your face!

> *(The SOLDIER obliges.)*

You! *(He gags.)* Christ!

SOLDIER: Is it the way I smell, sir?

DANCOCK: God ... yes!

SOLDIER: You're all in a sweat. Let me wipe your face.

DANCOCK: Get away from me! Don't touch me!

> *(The SOLDIER takes a handkerchief from his pocket and solicitously wipes DANCOCK's face.)*

SOLDIER: You're the last man I would have expected to find in such a predicament, sir. *(He tut tutts.)* What's the world coming to? *(He finishes wiping DANCOCK's face.)* There. That's better, isn't it? Of course, it is. *(Sniffs the handkerchief.)* What's this smell? *(Pause.)* Could it be the smell of fear? *(Implacable.)* Is it? Is it the smell of fear?

> *(He waits for an answer, but doesn't get one.)*

I stink, too. Don't I?

> *(DANCOCK is reluctant to answer. The SOLDIER asks louder.)*

Come now. What do I stink of?

DANCOCK: *(In a choked voice.)* The trenches. *(Pause.)* Mud. Blood. Shit. Rot.

SOLDIER: But not fear?

DANCOCK: No.

SOLDIER: Isn't that odd? Because I used to reek of it to high heaven. Didn't I, sir?

DANCOCK: Yes.

SOLDIER: But now you do.

DANCOCK: Yes.

SOLDIER: You're afraid. You can't move. Isn't that so?

DANCOCK: Yes.

SOLDIER: I couldn't move either. Frozen to the spot, wasn't I?

DANCOCK: Yes.

SOLDIER: They called you a hero. You had medals for bravery, didn't you, sir?

*(DANCOCK doesn't answer.)*

I'm sure there were medals.

DANCOCK: *(In a terrified whisper.)* What do you want?

SOLDIER: The question is, what do you want? *(Leaning over the bed, whispering seductively.)* Don't pretend it hasn't come into your mind once or twice.

*(He waits for a response. Getting none, he straightens up.)*

No? Well, think about it. Because in the end it all boils down to one simple question. What're you more afraid of? *(Indicates DANCOCK's surroundings.)* This? *(Suggestively.)* Or the dance? *(Pause.)* Maybe if I showed you a few steps it'd help you make up your mind. *(Cocking his ear.)* Listen!

*(Soft strains of "Mademoiselle from Armentieres" are heard. A weird, unearthly light floods the ward, revealing the SOLDIER, caked in mud, soaked in blood. He intently listens to the music, his finger marking time.)*

Oh, how I tripped the light fantastic in France. Do you recall, sir? *(Pause.)* Silly question. Of course you do!

*(The music swells and the SOLDIER dances, a dance of death. The dance lasts a brief moment and then the music breaks off.)*

*(Seductively.)* Come now, come clean. You want to dance. Admit it. *(Pause.)* And what a lovely dancer you'd make. Trust me.

*(Blackout.)*

## Scene Four

*(DOROTHEA GAGE is seated on a bench in intense sunshine. Her hands are folded in her lap, her eyes are closed, and her face is lifted to the sun, a vague smile on her lips. DANCOCK and KENNEALY enter. Not noticing her, they pause some distance from DOROTHEA, KENNEALY blabbing relentlessly at DANCOCK who is scarcely heeding what he says.)*

KENNEALY: Come, come, let's let bygones be bygones, Lieutenant. The Superintendent says strap you down and I straps you down. What else am I supposed to do?

DANCOCK: *(Catching sight of DOROTHEA.)* That girl there, Kennealy. Sitting on the bench under the tree. What's her name?

KENNEALY: How am I supposed to know the name of all eight hundred and fifty of youse?

DANCOCK: *(To himself.)* The girl from the dance. *(Decisively.)* Push off, Kennealy. I want a word alone with her.

KENNEALY: Can't oblige. The Superintendent appointed me your special guardian. With most definite instructions to see you don't go getting yourself excited. *(Pause.)* And if my eyes don't deceive me—that girl excites the Lieutenant.

DANCOCK: All right, what would it take for you to make yourself scarce?

KENNEALY: Open to offers.

DANCOCK: A dollar then. To take a stroll.

KENNEALY: Begging your pardon, sir. Touching on a delicate subject—your generous offer of a dollar for services previously rendered has yet to be honoured.

DANCOCK: All my money's held in the bursar's office. You know he'll only dole me out a few cents at a time so I can buy tobacco.

KENNEALY: There you have it. Exactly.

DANCOCK: You'll get every penny when I'm released—with interest.

KENNEALY: For a man in my position, a promise like that is a bit of a pig in a poke. There's some as never do get released from here.

*(DANCOCK is shaken.)*

KENNEALY: That's a lovely tie though. Silk is it?

DANCOCK: Silk. And in exchange?

KENNEALY: *(Glancing furtively about him.)* Thirty minutes and not a second more. I ought to have my Jesus head examined, but I'm a man same as you, Lieutenant, with a man's natural, human feelings.

*(DANCOCK unknots the tie.)*

Quick now! Before some Nosey Parker turns the corner!

*(DANCOCK hands him the tie and KENNEALY stuffs it in his smock.)*

*(As he sidles off.)* Thirty minutes and not a tick of the clock more! Do you hear me, Lieutenant! Thirty minutes!

*(KENNEALY exits. DANCOCK starts to approach the girl, looks at the condition of his hands, halts. He removes a pair of military style gloves from his jacket pocket and pulls them on, fussily smoothing down the leather. He glances at his hands once more and, satisfied, walks up to the bench. DOROTHEA's eyes are still closed. DANCOCK hesitates, fiddles with the gloves, collects himself to speak.)*

DANCOCK: Miss?

DOROTHEA: *(Starting.)* Heavens!

DANCOCK: Pardon! I've frightened you!

DOROTHEA: *(Smiling timidly.)* Not frightened—surprised.

DANCOCK: Forgiven?

*(DOROTHEA nods, smiles.)*

*(Indicating the bench.)* May I?

*(DOROTHEA shyly nods. DANCOCK prepares to take a seat.)*

DOROTHEA: Not so close!

*(DANCOCK, taken aback, rapidly shifts himself.)*

*(Explaining.)* In case I should ignite.

DANCOCK: Ignite?

DOROTHEA: *(Snapping her fingers.)* Poof!

DANCOCK: Poof?

DOROTHEA: It would be terrible if an innocent bystander were burned when I spontaneously combust. You do understand, don't you?

DANCOCK: *(Bewildered.)* Why ... I suppose ... *(Definitely.)* Yes. Yes I do.

DOROTHEA: *(Gratefully.)* I'm so glad! Because there's ever so many people who don't. They say I talk nonsense.

DANCOCK: *(Smiling.)* Well, that makes us a pair. People say I talk nonsense, too.

*(DOROTHEA returns his smile. He introduces himself.)*

John Dancock.

*(DOROTHEA refuses his hand in a way that makes it plain she is only doing so out of consideration for his safety. In case she should ignite.)*

DANCOCK: Oh, I see ...

DOROTHEA: Dorothea Gage.

*(A moment of shy, awkward silence.)*

DANCOCK: *(Abruptly.)* You don't recall me—

DOROTHEA: But I do! From the dance!

DANCOCK: Yes, the dance.

DOROTHEA: But you aren't a doctor.

DANCOCK: *(Laughing at the notion.)* Me! A doctor! Whatever gave you such an idea!

DOROTHEA: Because you asked me to dance. Patients mustn't invite other patients to dance. It's not allowed.

DANCOCK: Do you mind I'm not a doctor?

DOROTHEA: *(Gravely.)* No.

DANCOCK: *(Ardently.)* That blue gown of yours was a stunner.

DOROTHEA: It's for evening wear. But since there's no opportunities for evening parties ...

DANCOCK: Yes, being tucked in at seven o'clock does make an early night of it.

DOROTHEA: I haven't had such early nights since I was a small child.

DANCOCK: It looked splendid, your gown. *(A confession.)* It was happiness to look upon you.

*(DOROTHEA blushes, turns away.)*

Please ... please excuse my presumption, Miss Gage. You see, it's ages since I've conversed with a lady. I'm ... out of practice. *(Pause.)* Will you go again this week? To the dance I mean?

DOROTHEA: *(Turning back to him.)* I don't know ... You see, I go only for the music, to listen to the gramophone. *(Pause.)* I mustn't dance.

DANCOCK: Why mustn't you?

DOROTHEA: What if I were to burst into flames in someone's arms? It would be dreadful.

> *(DANCOCK nods.)*

The Superintendent claims I suffer from a *(She searches for the phrase.)* a fixed delusion. He says hay stacks may spontaneously combust, but not people. Now the Superintendent is a clever man, but Charles Dickens was a *genius* and he knew people did spontaneously combust. Have you read Bleak House?

DANCOCK: No, no I don't believe—

DOROTHEA: It's all in Bleak House. Mr. Dickens enumerates thirty cases of human spontaneous combustion, all attested to by eminent and distinguished professors. What has the Superintendent got to say to that!

> *(Having played her trump card, she is triumphant. The two sit quietly for a time, presumably meditating on spontaneous combustion.)*

*(Impulsively.)* I'm glad you're not a doctor!

DANCOCK: Why?

DOROTHEA: Because if you were a doctor you would argue with me that I am not going to combust. But being who you are, you know inexplicable things happen, because they have happened to you. *(Pause.)* Inexplicable things have happened to everyone here.

> *(DANCOCK nods to himself, mulling over this proposition.)*

DANCOCK: And how does it begin? This spontaneous combustion of yours?

DOROTHEA: It begins inside. You catch fire on the inside.

DANCOCK: Will there be a warning?

DOROTHEA: I have had warnings for years.

DANCOCK: And you aren't afraid?

*(DOROTHEA shakes her head. The SOLDIER enters and stands behind DANCOCK.)*

DANCOCK: *(Expressing his own fear.)* It's an ugly, nasty thing, fear. One of the dirtiest things there is. *(Pause.)* I'm so glad you aren't touched by it.

DOROTHEA: Well, perhaps we all are—just a little.

*(The SOLDIER lays a proprietorial hand on DANCOCK's shoulder. DANCOCK is afraid. The three stare out at the audience, as if posed for a turn-of-the-century photograph.)*

### Scene Five

*(The office of the SUPERINTENDENT. KENNEALY is seated on a chair. The SUPERINTENDENT is on his feet.)*

SUPERINTENDENT: I thought you would have recognized me for a determined man, Mr. Kennealy. Determined that my hospital set an example for all others of its kind. To help bring about the day when no more shame shall be attached to mental disease than to that of any other bodily organ. *(Pause.)* I was under the impression this was the aim of all of us who labour here.

KENNEALY: And so it is. No worries on that score. Not from Kennealy.

SUPERINTENDENT: And then I receive a report that you have solicited a patient.

KENNEALY: *(Warily.)* Soliciting in what wise, sir?

SUPERINTENDENT: An article of clothing.

KENNEALY: *(Thinking on his feet.)* Ah, Superintendent, the silk tie. Well, that was for his own good. The Lieutenant's face was dark as a storm cloud that day and I said to myself, "Kevin Kennealy," says I, "that poor devil has got it in mind to stretch his neck. Mark my words." So I relieved him of the very means of his selfsame destruction. But only for safekeeping, see. Kennealy's not the sort to traipse about with a silk tie knotted at his throat and his head in the clouds. By no means.

SUPERINTENDENT: *(Coldly.)* Not a tie. A suit of clothes.

KENNEALY: Who said such a thing? Braun! I suppose the Hun claims he was there! Liar!

SUPERINTENDENT: Take hold of yourself.

*(Rebuked, KENNEALY falls resentfully silent.)*

*(Passionately.)* Mr. Kennealy, my rules are not personal whims. They are based on scientific principles. Discipline is constructed with an eye to the welfare of the patients. When the inner world is disorder, chaos, rules provide a shape to their days, keep them in touch with ordinary life as it is lived outside these walls. That is why 850 patients rise at a given hour, eat at a given hour, retire at a given hour. That is why when a medical officer enters a ward, nurses and orderlies stand and remain standing until he departs. Not because my ego or my doctors' egos demand it, but as a symbol, as living proof to patients that all persons, staff included, must submit to discipline.

KENNEALY: And a great plan it is, sir.

SUPERINTENDENT: Provided staff set a good example. *(Pause.)* Begging from a patient is not a good example.

KENNEALY: *(False outrage.)* Beggar! Beggar! On the German's say so? *(Pause.)* I have always endeavoured to give satisfaction, sir.

SUPERINTENDENT: *(Exasperated.)* Endeavoured to give satisfaction! You are not a domestic servant, Mr. Kennealy. You are a healer of souls. A guide for the perplexed, a shoulder to lean upon for all these poor lost people robbed of reason, judgement, conscience—the things which make us human. *(Pause.)* But perhaps you do not agree.

KENNEALY: Sir?

SUPERINTENDENT: All these years I took it for granted that you and I were of one mind. But if that is not the case—then you had better seek employment elsewhere.

KENNEALY: *(Stunned.)* Turn me out? On the word of that German?

SUPERINTENDENT: Reform can never be carried forward by half-hearted men, Mr. Kennealy.

KENNEALY: Four years service and threaten a man with dismissal? It's not fair, sir.

SUPERINTENDENT: *(Pressing.)* Do you believe in what I am trying to accomplish in my hospital? Are we of one mind on this question?

*(KENNEALY stares at him.)*

*(Relentless.)* A simple question. Are we, or are we not of one mind?

KENNEALY: Of course, sir. Always have been. One mind.

SUPERINTENDENT: Good. That is all I wanted to hear. *(Pause.)* The tie. Give it back. *(Glances at his watch.)* I believe you are scheduled to supervise hydrotherapy at two o'clock. It is now five minutes to the hour.

> *(The SUPERINTENDENT resumes work. It is a dismissal. KENNEALY exits.)*

### Scene Six

> *(BRAUN is seated in an enclosed tub in the hydrotherapy room. The tub has a wooden cover cut down the middle lengthwise to make two doors. There is a hole in the cover through which BRAUN's head pokes. Beside the tub is a chair piled with BRAUN's clothes.)*

KENNEALY: *(Menacing.)* Been snitching? Playing teacher's pet? Telling tales out of school?

> *(BRAUN shakes his head desperately.)*

Somebody has.

BRAUN: Not Rudy.

KENNEALY: You told the Super about the suit.

BRAUN: No. Rudy said nothing about the suit.

KENNEALY: A little bird better not chirp in my ear you're lying. You know what happens when you lie to nice Mr. Kennealy.

BRAUN: I tell nothing about the suit!

KENNEALY: Or anything else.

BRAUN: Nothing else! I swear!

> *(KENNEALY prowls about the tub, an animal stalking prey. BRAUN cranes his neck anxiously, keeping him in view.)*

KENNEALY: Fucking Super, hauling me up on the carpet for "soliciting patients." As if everybody doesn't know how he landed in his soft bed. Licked some Liberal cabinet minister's arse until he struck honey. The old whore. Mr. High and Mighty Fancy Pants and Tinkle Tinkle China Balls. *(Does his impression of gentility.)* Ain't I the French poodle's bum!

*(BRAUN laughs because he thinks it is expected of him. KENNEALY turns on him.)*

Who you laughing at?

*(BRAUN shrinks down in the tub.)*

Me? You laughing at me?

*(He grabs BRAUN by the hair and violently shakes his head from side to side.)*

Kennealy a joke, is that it? Is that it! Is that it!

*(KENNEALY thrusts BRAUN's head away from him. BRAUN whimpers.)*

So I'm a beggar, am I? Then what are you, boyo? Three squares a day, roof over your head, toasty steam heat, games, dances—all at public expense. And Kevin Kennealy to wipe and powder your arse for you, if the need arises. My thanks, my reward? The holy, blessed joy of twelve hour days, six days a week. Side pork for supper, shiver in a shack, varicose veins. And mind your manners, says his nibs, or bloody piss off. *(Pause.)* And he wants me to love you besides?

BRAUN: Please, Mr. Kennealy, let me out the bath. I want out, please. I'm clean now.

KENNEALY: Clean? You, clean, you piece of shit? Filth is what you are. Filth outside and in.

BRAUN: *(Pleading.)* Kind Mr. Kennealy ... please.

KENNEALY: Stable sweepings.

BRAUN: *(Making a timid, ineffectual effort to assert himself.)* I am the king. The king says for you to let him out.

KENNEALY: The king are you? Where's your crown, king? A king has to have a crown.

BRAUN: Let me out. Please, Mr. Kennealy.

*(KENNEALY takes off one of his elastic sleeve garters and slips it around BRAUN's brow.)*

KENNEALY: There's a crown for you! *(Begins to salaam.)* All hail, king of the loonies! All hail!

BRAUN: *(Terrified.)* Rudy's clean now! Let him out! Give him his clothes!

KENNEALY: I'll give you your clothes!

*(KENNEALY snatches up BRAUN's clothes and flings them in his face. When he does, a bouquet of flowers hidden among them is revealed.)*

*(Seizing them.)* What's this, what's this?

BRAUN: Blumen! Flowers! Lieutenant Dancock says to Rudy, "Pick me the wild flowers when you go to work on the farm. For each flower you bring I pay you one cigarette."

KENNEALY: What's he want with flowers?

BRAUN: To make a present. For Miss Gage.

KENNEALY: Playing cupid are we, Rudy? Isn't that sweet?

*(KENNEALY takes the flowers and begins to arrange them in the garter about BRAUN's head.)*

Now you look a proper cupid. Lovely little cupid. Cupid with his wings clipped.

BRAUN: Let me out! I'm clean now! Rudy's clean.

KENNEALY: *(Suggestive, sinister.)* I know better. Don't I?

BRAUN: Let me out! Rudy's clean!

KENNEALY: Not clean. Filthy. You're a filthy boy, Rudy. *(He begins to pluck the flowers, one by one.)* He loves me, he loves me not, he loves me, he loves me not …

BRAUN: *(Struggling to free himself from the locked tub.)* NO!

*(KENNEALY slaps him.)*

BRAUN: NO!

*(KENNEALY slaps him again. BRAUN begins to weep helplessly, hopelessly. KENNEALY unbuttons his flies, straddles the bathtub, and seats himself on the boards facing BRAUN.)*

KENNEALY: *(Sliding himself towards BRAUN.)* Come on then. Come on then. Come on!

### Scene Seven

*(DOROTHEA stands beside the bench in bright sunlight, looking up. Muted bird song. DANCOCK enters. DOROTHEA remains perfectly still, face tilted to the sky. DANCOCK hurriedly pulls on his gloves before approaching her. Without looking at him, she signals he is standing too near. He edges away, then turns his face upward also.)*

DANCOCK: What are we looking for?

DOROTHEA: *(Still looking up.)* Birds.

*(They study the tree tops.)*

DANCOCK: You like birds?

*(DOROTHEA looks at him, nods fervently. They return to searching the tree tops.)*

Tell me, how is it that you are always alone, without an attendant? For the rest of us, it isn't allowed.

DOROTHEA: I'm voluntary. I agreed to come here. *(Pause.)* So they trust me.

DANCOCK: *(Sceptical.)* Agreed?

DOROTHEA: Mother thought it would be best. Father found my spontaneous combustion business most upsetting. He's not well, you know. His heart. *(Pause.)* It was more convenient for all concerned.

DANCOCK: *(With dismay and disbelief.)* More convenient?

DOROTHEA: Yes. It is inconvenient to be where you are not wanted. *(Pause.)* And you, Mr. Dancock? How is it that you are without an attendant?

DANCOCK: I bribe him.

DOROTHEA: *(Delighted.)* Really! With what!

DANCOCK: Today ... *(He shoots his cuffs and exposes unfastened French cuffs.)* Voila! Cuff links.

DOROTHEA: No!

DANCOCK: Silver cuff links for half an hour alone with you.

DOROTHEA: You pay too high a price for my company. *(Believing what she says.)* I am not worth it.

DANCOCK: You most certainly are.

DOROTHEA: Please do not speak of it.

DANCOCK: *(Realizing she is upset.)* Since I am forbidden to speak my mind, then you must set the topic of conversation.

DOROTHEA: *(Mood swinging. Teasing.)* Birds.

DANCOCK: Birds is it? *(An exaggeration of polite parlour conversation.)* My dear Miss Gage, of all our feathered friends, of all the carollers of the bright empyrean blue, which is your favourite fowl? *(Pause.)* If I might be so bold as to inquire?

(*DOROTHEA hesitates.*)

She is at a loss for words. (*Pause.*) My particular affection is for the barn owl because he bears such a striking resemblance to our own Superintendent.

DOROTHEA: Mine is the phoenix.

DANCOCK: The phoenix?

DOROTHEA: Yes.

DANCOCK: You mean the mythical bird—

DOROTHEA: (*With serene conviction.*) It lives ever so long, all alone, and when it's five hundred years old it builds a beautiful nest of the rarest spices and it sits on the nest and sings a sad song and flaps its wings and flaps its wings until the nest catches fire and the flames burst up all about it and the spices catch fire and a wonderful scent like nothing else on earth fills the air, and the phoenix is consumed, singing, until there is nothing but ashes. (*Pause.*) And out of the ashes ... a new phoenix is born.

DANCOCK: It sounds a beautiful bird—to hear you tell it. It's as if you've seen it.

DOROTHEA: I have.

DANCOCK: (*Carefully.*) Have you.

DOROTHEA: Do you want to see it too? Look there. (*She points, lifts her gaze to the sun.*) Into the sun. Look, with your eyes opened wide.

DANCOCK: (*Tries, but has to avert his eyes.*) It's too bright.

DOROTHEA: Look into the heart of the fire. Just a moment.

(*DANCOCK manages.*)

Now close your eyes.

(*Both of them close their eyes.*)

Do you see it? The dark shape moving in the flames. Wings rising and falling. Do you see it?

DANCOCK: I ... I'm not sure.

DOROTHEA: Look! Look hard! Now do you see it!

DANCOCK: I—

DOROTHEA: The dark form, in the heart of all the bright light. (*Pleading.*) You do see it! Don't you?

DANCOCK: (*He opens his eyes and looks at her.*) Now ... yes. I do.

*(DOROTHEA opens her eyes.)*

DOROTHEA: *(Exalted.)* There!

DANCOCK: *(Slightly guilty.)* Does it matter so very much to you that I should see it too?

DOROTHEA: Yes.

> *(DANCOCK waits for her to say more. She doesn't. She believes he understands.)*

DANCOCK: Will you come to the dance tomorrow?

DOROTHEA: I ... I cannot promise, Mr. Dancock.

DANCOCK: Please come. I must see you.

DOROTHEA: Why must you see me?

DANCOCK: Because you remind me of ...

DOROTHEA: Of what?

DANCOCK: Of what I once was.

DOROTHEA: And what was that?

DANCOCK: A different man. Happier. Better. *(Pause.)* When war began, a politician said, "The lamps are going out all over Europe; we shall not see them lit again in our lifetime." The old men have condemned the young to live in darkness. But when I look at you, I believe in the possibility of light.

DOROTHEA: Lieutenant Dancock ...

DANCOCK: *(Interrupting desperately.)* The voice that warns you of the fire to come. Do you see it?

> *(DOROTHEA shakes her head.)*

No? *(Bewildered.)* I see a voice. It entreats me to go with it—

> *(The SOLDIER enters.)*

DOROTHEA: Go with it where?

DANCOCK: I don't want to go with it. But I am afraid I will ... unless ...

DOROTHEA: Unless what?

> *(DANCOCK puts his head in his hands. The SOLDIER steals up on DOROTHEA from behind and rests his hands on her shoulders. She feels something, reacts to the presence. DANCOCK begins to weep. Moved, DOROTHEA reaches out to touch his head, but withdraws it, afraid she might ignite. The*

*SOLDIER begins to caress her cheek and neck. She feels him more strongly. DOROTHEA reaches out to DANCOCK impulsively, but cannot bring herself to touch him. The SOLDIER continues to fondle her.)*

DANCOCK: *(Ashamed.)* Please excuse me. You must excuse me.

*(He looks up, sees the SOLDIER touching DOROTHEA and is horrified.)*

Stop it!

DOROTHEA: *(Alarmed by DANCOCK's reaction.)* What is it, Mr. Dancock? What is the matter?

*(The SOLDIER smiles, caressing her triumphantly.)*

SOLDIER: Everything you touch, Dancock, I touch too.

DANCOCK: STOP IT!

### Scene Eight

*(Dance music of the period is heard, mingled with the sounds of conversation in a crowded room. A few chairs are scattered around the margins of the dance floor. On a table a wind-up gramophone and punch bowl rest. The SUPERINTENDENT and KENNEALY stand beside the table, talking and watching the dancers whom the audience must imagine and who are treated by the actors as real and present. DANCOCK and BRAUN stand on the other side of the room; DANCOCK anxiously watching the door for sign of DOROTHEA.)*

BRAUN: *(Pointing at an imaginary couple.)* Lieutenant! Lieutenant! Look at Mr. Decker! Maybe we put some turpentine on Mr. Decker's ass, he really waltz! *(He crouches and scoots his ass around like a dog dragging it through the dirt.)* Ja!

DANCOCK: *(Scarcely heeding BRAUN and his performance.)* Where is Miss Gage?

BRAUN: Maybe Rudy should ask the Matron to dance? Or maybe it is not fair to raise Matron's hopes since Rudy is married? *(He waggles his fingers across the room to Matron. Then tugs at DANCOCK's sleeve.)* See! The Matron is studying the leaves of the plant when Rudy waves hello. What is the English for that?

DANCOCK: For what?

BRAUN: To refuse to catch the eye of the attractive male?

DANCOCK: Flirtation.

BRAUN: So, the matron is doing a flirtation on Rudy.

DANCOCK: *(Speaking of DOROTHEA.)* Where can she be?

BRAUN: Behind the plant. Matron is behind the plant. See? Hiding ever deeper in the love flirtation with Rudy.

DANCOCK: I felt sure Miss Gage would come.

BRAUN: *(Depression surfacing.)* The Superintendent recommends the dancing for the low spirits. Rudy has been feeling bugger low. *(Pause.)* You think Rudy should dance a little?

DANCOCK: *(Impatiently.)* By all means. Off you go and dance, Rudy.

BRAUN: *(Afraid to venture off by himself.)* You, too, Lieutenant? You will dance also?

DANCOCK: *(Distracted.)* Me? No, not now. If Miss Gage arrives … we shall see.

BRAUN: *(Tugging at his arm.)* Show Rudy how it is done to invite proper the English nurses. Maybe we should both go and dance together with the English nurses.

DANCOCK: Stop pulling at my sleeve! If you want to dance— dance! If not, get yourself a bloody glass of lemonade and leave me alone!

BRAUN: *(Distraught.)* You should come with. They are very severe, the English nurses. I do not know how they like to be invited to dance. Come and show Rudy how to do it!

> *(KENNEALY takes his leave of the SUPERINTENDENT and begins to make his way towards BRAUN and DANCOCK.)*

DANCOCK: Here's Kennealy. Ask him how to do it. I hear he's quite the Don Juan.

> *(BRAUN takes one look at KENNEALY and scuttles off to the punch bowl and the SUPERINTENDENT.)*

KENNEALY: Where's the sauerkraut farter off to in such a hurry?

DANCOCK: Look here, Kennealy, have you seen Miss Gage?

KENNEALY: *(With a knowing smile.)* Little Miss Alice Blue Gown? Not today I haven't.

DANCOCK: *(Anxiously.)* Where can she have got to? If she doesn't come soon the dance'll be over!

KENNEALY: *(Surveying the dancers.)* Is that Nurse Jones? Sweet crumpet, Nursie Jones, lick the marmelade and the butter off her, I would. Who's that she's dancing with? Billings? *(Outraged.)* Bloody Billings! Birthday Billings, swears every day's his birthday and pesters me for cake! Christ, there's a birthday party for you, pushing it up against Nursie Jones. Disgusting! The Super shouldn't allow it, that sort of thing.

> *(Just then DOROTHEA makes her entrance, resplendent in a blue ball gown. She crosses the room, making her way through the imaginary dancers to a chair where she sits, hands demurely folded in her lap. DANCOCK and DOROTHEA gaze across the room at one another. DANCOCK prepares to cross to her, but KENNEALY seizes his arm.)*

No. *(Inclines his head towards the SUPERINTENDENT who has noticed nothing, being deep in conversation with BRAUN.)* Not in front of the governor.

> *(DANCOCK removes KENNEALY's hand and proceeds to DOROTHEA.)*

Don't look for trouble!

DANCOCK: *(Offering her his hand.)* Miss Gage ...

> *(DANCOCK catches sight of the scabs on his hand, hurriedly withdraws it and pulls on his leather gloves.)*

Excuse me ... I ... an oversight—

DOROTHEA: Oughtn't they to be white?

DANCOCK: Pardon?

DOROTHEA: For dancing, ought not a gentleman wear white gloves? And if not white gloves, then none at all?

DANCOCK: Strictly speaking, I believe that is so—

DOROTHEA: Do not think me rude. I am not in the least experienced. My father did not approve of dancing. Of course, it would be irresponsible of me to dance with a man, whether his hands were protected from burns or not.

DANCOCK: My dear Miss Gage! I was not protecting myself from you but rather you from me! *(Struggling to explain.)* My hands ... are an ugly mess. They ... bleed!

*(The SUPERINTENDENT sees DANCOCK talking to DOROTHEA and moves to intervene. KENNEALY hastens to his side. )*

*(Struggling through his embarrassment.)* Nevertheless, I mean to say—*(Drawing himself together.)* I mean to say, would you do me the very great honour of dancing with me, Miss Gage?

SUPERINTENDENT: *(Having arrived just in time.)* Keep your seat, Miss Gage.

DANCOCK: How dare you speak to a lady in that fashion! Apologize at once!

SUPERINTENDENT: Do not test me, Lieutenant. Come away at once!

*(The SUPERINTENDENT takes DANCOCK by the arm but DANCOCK violently shakes him off and turns back to DOROTHEA.)*

DANCOCK: Miss Gage, if I might have the … pleasure of this dance.

SUPERINTENDENT: *(Signalling to KENNEALY.)* Take him out.

*(KENNEALY catches hold of him from behind.)*

DANCOCK: *(Speaking to DOROTHEA as if his life depends on it.)* If … if you would dance with me!

KENNEALY: Be a good chap. No fuss, please. A bit of a lie down is what you want.

DANCOCK: *(Exploding.)* Take your hands off me! I am speaking to Miss Gage!

KENNEALY: Don't make a fool of yourself in front of the lady. Best to go calm, quiet and dignified like.

*(The advice puts DANCOCK over the edge. A violent struggle ensues. KENNEALY manages to gain control of him with an arm lock and forces him out of the door, DANCOCK raging. DOROTHEA is terribly upset. )*

SUPERINTENDENT: *(Addressing the imaginary dancers.)* Ladies and gentlemen, if you would return to your seats, just for the moment. No need to be alarmed. Lieutenant Dancock is in good hands. I know how upsetting this has been for you all. I can assure you Lieutenant Dancock will be barred from future tea dances—

*(KENNEALY enters, the SUPERINTENDENT breaks off in surprise. DOROTHEA is near enough to them to hear DANCOCK being discussed.)*

Mr. Kennealy?

KENNEALY: I've turned him over to Mr. Markham and Mr. Struthers.

SUPERINTENDENT: As you see fit. *(Turning back to the imaginary dancers.)* Ladies and gentlemen—

KENNEALY: Begging your pardon, Superintendent.

SUPERINTENDENT: What, Mr. Kennealy!

KENNEALY: If I might make a suggestion about the patient?

SUPERINTENDENT: Go on.

KENNEALY: *(Definitely.)* I'd have him put in a cage bed. Recommended for violent cases, the cage bed is.

SUPERINTENDENT: You consider Dancock a violent case?

KENNEALY: He's uttering threats, sir.

SUPERINTENDENT: Against whom?

KENNEALY: Yourself, sir. Myself.

SUPERINTENDENT: I think we can take care of ourselves. Don't you?

KENNEALY: Only thinking of the hospital's good name, sir. *(Pause.)* Wouldn't want him harming another patient. Or himself. *(Pause.)* Wouldn't want a scandal.

*(The SUPERINTENDENT considers.)*

He's fair wild, sir.

SUPERINTENDENT: All right, the cage bed. For tonight only.

KENNEALY: Very good, sir.

*(KENNEALY exits.)*

BRAUN: *(Stepping forward to confront the SUPERINTENDENT.)* Super ... Super ... Super ...

*(Agitated and unable to get out what he wants to say, he bursts into tears and rushes from the room.)*

SUPERINTENDENT: *(To DOROTHEA.)* Miss Gage, my most sincere apologies for any embarrassment this incident may have caused you. But let me set your mind at rest on this point. I know that you had no hand in Dancock's mischief—

DOROTHEA: Mischief! How can it be mischief to ask a lonely soul to dance? It did not feel like mischief. It felt like kindness.

SUPERINTENDENT: Miss Gage, you do not comprehend what is at issue here.

DOROTHEA: The cage bed is at issue here. A man kept like a dog in a kennel. Shame on you.

SUPERINTENDENT: Miss Gage, this is unlike you. You are not yourself.

DOROTHEA: You, sir, are not yourself. You are behaving like a jailer. Not like a doctor.

SUPERINTENDENT: Be so good as to remember that I have my hospital to protect.

DOROTHEA: And Mr. Dancock? Who protects him?

SUPERINTENDENT: *(Stung by this remark.)* I beg you to please sit down.

DOROTHEA: I think not. It feels good to stand. I will stand until you return Mr. Dancock to us.

SUPERINTENDENT: Are you forgetting? It is I who am in charge here.

DOROTHEA: Are you forgetting? I am a voluntary patient.

SUPERINTENDENT: If it is for your own good, Miss Gage, your status can easily be changed. If I were to so advise, your father would sign the necessary papers of committal.

*(DOROTHEA is taken aback. A moment of indecision, and then she chooses.)*

DOROTHEA: Let him sign then. Let him sign.

*(DOROTHEA brushes by the SUPERINTENDENT and makes a dignified exit.)*

### Scene Nine

*(Dancock's room. Dim light, just strong enough to make out a bed mounted with an iron cage resembling a huge lobster trap. The SOLDIER enters, saunters up to the cage bed with a swagger stick in his hand.)*

DANCOCK: *(From inside the cage.)* Is that you?

SOLDIER: Who else? I'm not done with you yet, old son. Not by a long shot.

> *(The SOLDIER prowls about the cage, halts and holds the swagger stick above the bars.)*

Recognize this?

DANCOCK: Yes.

SOLDIER: *(Harshly.)* What is it? Say what it is.

DANCOCK: A swagger stick.

SOLDIER: Whose swagger stick?

> *(DANCOCK refuses to answer. The SOLDIER taps the bars with the stick.)*

Whose?

DANCOCK: MINE!

SOLDIER: A swagger stick for a swaggering bastard. You were a swaggering bastard, weren't you? Batman to shine your kit for you every morning. Sam Brown belt polished. High boots polished. Quite the shiny, swaggering boy you were.

DANCOCK: Go away. Let me sleep.

SOLDIER: And now you play the great friend of the downtrodden. Rights of man and all that crap. Flaming Bolshie.

DANCOCK: Let me alone.

SOLDIER: *(Suddenly sniffs the air like a dog.)* What's that I smell? Is that stink coming from in there …?

DANCOCK: Keep away from me!

SOLDIER: Did Shiny Swaggering Boy dirty his cot? Foul his nest? Shame.

DANCOCK: I called and called but Kennealy didn't come! I couldn't hold it!

SOLDIER: And now you have to lie in it all night.

DANCOCK: *(Pleading.)* You could let me out. Let me out, why don't you?

SOLDIER: *(Looking around him.)* Not many people get let out of here. They hold you for just as long as they fancy. People die old in places like this.

DANCOCK: That's a lie!

SOLDIER: It's the truth. *(Pause.)* Held at His Majesty's pleasure it's called. *(Pause.)* Meaning the Superintendent's pleasure.

DANCOCK: I'll get out of here! Soon!

SOLDIER: The problem with your type is you don't know how to bend. They don't like that in places like this—men who won't bend.

DANCOCK: You'll see! I'll get out!

SOLDIER: You don't really believe that, do you? No, sir, you're here for a very long time. Years and years, I'd say. *(Pause.)* Locked up, trapped, buried alive—

DANCOCK: *(Interrupting.)* Please!

SOLDIER: A lifetime of slow rot. Bad as the trenches. Worse maybe. *(Pause.)* What would you say, sir? Is it worse?

DANCOCK: Leave me alone!

SOLDIER: Is it?

   *(DANCOCK doesn't answer.)*

Worse than the trenches?

DANCOCK: Yes, goddamn it!

SOLDIER: And only one way out. *(Pause.)* Dance your way out.

   *(Silence.)*

I took my turn. Now it's yours.

DANCOCK: *(Hollow voiced.)* No.

SOLDIER: You needn't dance like me. Oh no. Dance like an officer if you please. To each his own. All the better.

   *(DANCOCK begins to sob.)*

Come now, no tears. Tears don't change the facts. I learned that.

DANCOCK: *(In a fury.)* You son of a bitch!

SOLDIER: *(Offering his hand.)* Take my hand. Take it and dance. *(Waits.)* No? *(Pause.)* All right, as you wish. Shake the bars of your dog kennel. Lie in your own shit. Howl at the moon. It won't do you any good because nobody but me is listening. *(With utter contempt.)* If you could only see yourself, how low you've sunk. *(Pause.)* I'll leave you to rot then.

   *(The SOLDIER appears to be on the point of exiting, but then he stops, waits for what he knows will happen, his back to DANCOCK and the cage. DANCOCK's hand rises through the*

*bars of the cage, hesitantly. It freezes in mid-air, an appeal. The SOLDIER, even though his back is turned to DANCOCK smiles triumphantly, knowing he has succeeded. He turns back to the bed and holds out his hand, just beyond the reach of DANCOCK's fingers. DANCOCK must strain to reach it and when he does, the SOLDIER grips it triumphantly.)*

It's begun then! The dance has begun!

*(Blackout.)*

## Act Two

### *Scene One*

*(The SUPERINTENDENT and KENNEALY in the SUPERIN-TENDENT's office.)*

SUPERINTENDENT: Where's Lieutenant Dancock now?

KENNEALY: He's outside in the corridor. Murdoch's keeping an eye on him while we talk.

SUPERINTENDENT: Exactly how long has it been since he started refusing all food?

KENNEALY: Fifteen days, sir.

SUPERINTENDENT: And in that time he's taken nothing?

KENNEALY: Just as you say, sir.

SUPERINTENDENT: This is what I get for locking a proud man in a cage bed. He's done nothing but deteriorate ever since that night. *(Pause.)* I'm not going to lose this man. He's not going to be allowed to starve himself to death.

KENNEALY: Then you better force feed him.

SUPERINTENDENT: No. Not yet. God knows how he'd react. It's a humiliating business, having slop poured into you through a funnel. He might withdraw even further.

KENNEALY: He might die if you don't.

SUPERINTENDENT: I know, I know. *(He pauses, thinking.)* He hasn't spoken either?

KENNEALY: Not a peep out of him to me.

SUPERINTENDENT: And nothing to me. Still I'm convinced it's not a case of developing catatonia. Something about the eyes ... You're certain he speaks to no one? No one at all?

KENNEALY: Well ...

SUPERINTENDENT: *(Eagerly.)* Yes?

KENNEALY: I've come on the ward and found Braun jabbering at him. But the German clams up whenever he spots me. I've never seen Dancock answer him.

SUPERINTENDENT: Braun, eh? Yes, it's possible. *(Suddenly.)* Bring Dancock in, Mr. Kennealy.

KENNEALY: Very good, sir.

> *(KENNEALY exits. He returns with DANCOCK who shuffles into the room, haggard, blank. KENNEALY steers him to an empty chair where DANCOCK sits woodenly, staring straight ahead.)*

SUPERINTENDENT: Thank you, Mr. Kennealy. You may leave.

> *(KENNEALY exits. The SUPERINTENDENT moves a chair so he can sit nearer his patient.)*

You can speak if you choose to. Your eyes give you away, Dancock. What's the phrase? Windows of the soul? You look out at us, but we are not permitted to look in at you. But I want to look in. *(Pause.)* Perhaps you would tell me about the war.

> *(DANCOCK refuses to answer. The SOLDIER enters.)*

SOLDIER: He wants to learn about the war. Wants a peek in those windows of yours. Are you going to let him in?

> *(Throughout this scene, the SUPERINTENDENT does not see the SOLDIER, neither does he hear or react to what DANCOCK says to the SOLDIER. As far as he is concerned, DANCOCK is mute.)*

I wouldn't either. Fucking snoop. You don't owe him an explanation.

SUPERINTENDENT: I'm not a man without imagination. I can guess what it was like.

SOLDIER: Imagination? Yes, but only when he's playing with his dick.

SUPERINTENDENT: Your record makes clear you were an admirable officer.

> *(The SOLDIER laughs.)*

DANCOCK: *(Speaking to the SOLDIER, ignoring the SUPERINTENDENT.)* I did my best.

SOLDIER: For your superiors.

DANCOCK: No, for my men! I wrote letters home for the illiterates, gave characters for those brought up on charges, saw that the quartermaster didn't cheat them on rations and blankets—

SOLDIER: Three cheers for you.

DANCOCK: It was more than many officers did!

SUPERINTENDENT: Just a word. One word, Lieutenant.

DANCOCK: I cared for my men.

SOLDIER: Your men? You make it sound as if you owned them, body and soul.

DANCOCK: I loved my men.

SOLDIER: But feared failure more.

DANCOCK: When an officer fails, he fails his men.

SOLDIER: Bullshit. Those young officers who were born with silver spoons in their cake holes and who blew their brains out when their men refused orders—why did they do it? Not because they failed the muckers under them who said, "I've had enough of getting shot to shit for King and Country" but because they'd failed the big shots who decide when it is and isn't time to die for King and Country. *(Pause.)* And you were no different from them.

*(DANCOCK doesn't answer.)*

SUPERINTENDENT: *(Earnestly.)* My methods work. Give them a chance. I can help you. I want to help you.

SOLDIER: Officers love their men like they do their dogs. When they're devoted. When they come smartly to heel. There's always a little contempt mixed in. *(Pause.)* But it's a poor sort of man who can't win the love of a dog. Maybe that's what had those officers blowing their brains out.

SUPERINTENDENT: All right. We needn't talk just yet. But allow me to sit and keep you company awhile.

*(The SUPERINTENDENT takes his hand.)*

SOLDIER: *(To DANCOCK.)* And whose dog are you?

### Scene Two

*(DOROTHEA, DANCOCK, and the SUPERINTENDENT stand in pools of light. They address the audience.)*

SUPERINTENDENT: I have long realized this day might come—a day when I would be called to answer before the bar of public opinion. A crisis looms and I know what will be said of me, later, when this sad and sorry business has come to an end. You will have read reports in this morning's newspaper about the spread of Spanish influenza, 20 million dead in Europe and Asia, 20,000 cases in Montreal. You will have heard rumours of isolated farmsteads in which the dead are found lying in every room of the house, and the survivors wander the fields, out of their minds with fever.

DANCOCK: Yesterday it suddenly came over me again, how it was, the one impossibly bright, shining moment which stabs your heart for the rest of your life. Which whispers to you that everything has changed.

DOROTHEA: *(Humbly.)* My father is a good father, an instructive father. Young ladies do not ride bicycles, he said. It is vulgar.

DANCOCK: Marching to the troop ships! Christ, the crowds, the cheering! A froth of tiny Union Jacks quivering in the air like butterflies. I've never seen more happiness gathered in one spot in my life—not at a wedding, not at a Charlie Chaplin movie, not anywhere.

DOROTHEA: Young ladies do not go to the movies, he said. It is corrupting. Young ladies do not work for wages in shops and banks. It is demeaning. Young ladies do not dance. It is frivolous.

DANCOCK: A great wave of stupid happiness and I was drunk with it. Not because they were cheering me, but because they were cheering my boys!

DOROTHEA: Young ladies do keep the fourth commandment, "Honour thy father and thy mother, all the days of your life." My father is a good father, an instructive father.

SUPERINTENDENT: In some towns, armed guards have been posted at the train station to prevent passengers from disembarking and spreading the infection. It isn't working. It is only a matter of time before the Spanish influenza reaches my hospital.

DANCOCK: By God, my boys looked good that day! They'd never marched on any parade ground the way they marched that day! Sixty pairs of boots striking the road like one boot, a joyous animal with a single spine, a single brain, a single will! And me in perfect step with them!

SUPERINTENDENT: My most experienced orderlies and nurses were recruited for overseas. The Government did not replace them. In four years our patient population has increased from 346 to 850. The Spanish flu will sweep through our overcrowded wards like a prairie fire.

DOROTHEA: Every evening I read aloud to father. As the poet Milton's daughters did for him. Walter Scott was a great favourite of his. Browning, Shakespeare, Wilkie Collins. He loved Dickens. I read him the collected works of Dickens.

SUPERINTENDENT: Hundreds of my patients are certain to die.

DOROTHEA: And all those years Father assumed that the words went in my eyes and out my mouth, without ever passing through my brain. *(Pause.)* Curious, isn't it?

SUPERINTENDENT: I lobbied the Government to build me an isolation ward. I said without it, any outbreak of infectious disease would have dire consequences. I was accused of crying wolf. I begged them. "Next year," they promised. But next year never came. *(Pause.)* But now it has come.

DANCOCK: I took this as a sign they accepted me, accepted my leadership. Their confidence was a great gift to me because I had disappointed so often before—at school, in my father's business. But that day they gave me something, something that bloody took my breath away!

SUPERINTENDENT: So do not lay responsibility for what is going to happen at my door! It is not my doing! Do you hear me! Not mine!

DANCOCK: And just then, young Private Watkins looks over at me and says, "We'll go through that old Kaiser like shit through a goose, won't we, sir!" And smiled. A strange, innocent, trusting smile.

SUPERINTENDENT: I yearned to accomplish something great, something noble in my hospital.

DANCOCK: A boy wanting to be reassured that all would be well. I smiled back.

SUPERINTENDENT: I yearned to lead men and women out of torment, out of darkness and into the light.

DOROTHEA: When I was sixteen I read an article in the newspaper about a coal mine which had caught fire and had been burning for six years. No one and nothing could put it out.

SUPERINTENDENT: And for those I could not return to the light I wished to provide a sanctuary from all that had bruised and broken them in the hard world outside. I yearned to do these things!

DOROTHEA: Deep underground it burned, under a suffocating weight of earth, little tongues of fire licking into nooks and crannies, black veins of coal pulsing with heat! While over top it, fields of corn, pastures, red barns, little white unsuspecting houses!

DANCOCK: We turned a corner in the street and there was the harbour, the boats, the water so blue it hurt your eyes. And at the sight of that vast sheet of blue the men began to sing with one voice. Tipperary. I joined in. *(A confession.)* I would have died for them.

SUPERINTENDENT: But my sanctuary has proved a death trap.

DANCOCK: Someone once said every man and woman must experience a moment, the sweetness of which would lead them to willingly relive their whole life again, all the monotony, all the misery, for the sake of that one moment. On the way to that shining blue harbour I believed I had seized, or been seized by my bright moment. *(Pause.)* It was a lie.

SUPERINTENDENT: Down the corridor a young man is slowly starving himself to death. Who is responsible?

DOROTHEA: And I wonder this: How does that subterranean, hidden, secret fire burn for years and years without air?

### Scene Three

*(The SUPERINTENDENT strides angrily across the stage, KENNEALY trailing after him apologetically.)*

SUPERINTENDENT: Damn it, how could such a thing happen!

KENNEALY: Begging your pardon, sir. We didn't know.

SUPERINTENDENT: Four women out of their heads with fever, raving, and you didn't know!

KENNEALY: Well, they often rave—so how were we to know?

SUPERINTENDENT: That's why you were given thermometers. To take temperatures. Three of those women register 103 and one of them 104.

KENNEALY: *(Frightened.)* Is it the flu, sir?

SUPERINTENDENT: *(Briskly.)* They must be put in quarantine. How many patients are now in the infirmary?

KENNEALY: Just Dancock, sir.

SUPERINTENDENT: We'll convert the infirmary to an isolation ward. Move Dancock out. In his weakened condition he won't stand a chance if exposed to the flu. *(Thinking.)* Maybe the time has come to force feed him. In this situation further delay could be his death sentence. *(Making a decision.)* Start tonight. *(Gathering energy.)* Distribute surgical masks to staff. No one enters quarantine without wearing one. *(Sharply.)* Just don't stand there, man! Get a move on!

*(The SUPERINTENDENT exits.)*

KENNEALY: *(Resentful.)* I might get a move on, move on out of this bloody place if I had anywhere else to go. So don't push me, see. *(Yells.)* Just don't push me!

*(KENNEALY exits.)*

### Scene Four

*(DANCOCK is sitting on a hard-backed chair in his room. He is unkempt, obviously depressed and relentlessly scratching his hands. BRAUN enters carrying something wrapped in a linen napkin.)*

BRAUN: *(Calling in a low voice.)* Herr Lieutenant. I have come. Herr Lieutenant. Yoohoo. Yoohoo.

*(DANCOCK doesn't acknowledge BRAUN's presence. He continues scraping at his hands with his nails. BRAUN rushes over and tries to stop him.)*

Stop it! Stop! Superintendent comes and puts the bandages on your hands and you tear them off. Where are the bandages? *(He searches for them and finds them on the bed, stained with blood.)* Here, here. Let Rudy wrap your hands. *(He winds the bandages clumsily around DANCOCK's hands, scolding him as he does.)* This is not a nice thing you do. Superintendent says do not do it. Rudy says do not do it. Yet you, you pisser, you do it!

*(DANCOCK holds up the bandaged hands and stares at them.)*

Do not look at them! Look at me! I am talking to you! Look at Rudy!

*(DANCOCK looks at him.)*

Ja, at Rudy. Because Rudy has come to pay the visit. I sneak up the backstairs, I sneak down the hall way, I sneak like the little mouse to say hello to my friend. *(Holding up the bundle.)* Up the backstairs, down the hall way, look what comes with Rudy. Guess.

*(When DANCOCK doesn't guess, BRAUN nevertheless carries on cheerfully.)*

Before he was a king, Rudy was a baker. A good baker. So the Superintendent puts him to work in the Hospital bakery. *(Pulls a face in disgust.)* The English bread is all air and bad smells. Like a fart. *(Pause.)* But for you, I make a special loaf. The German bread. *(Unfolding the napkin.)* Hot just this minute from the oven. I wrap him up to keep him hot for you. Ja?

*(DANCOCK remains distant, in his own world. BRAUN holds the small loaf to DANCOCK's cheek.)*

Feel how warm. Soft and warm like a titty. *(Thrusting the loaf under his nose.)* Smell!

*(DANCOCK pushes it away.)*

*(Persisting.)* Fresh and hot. I brought for you a little butter twisted up in paper in my pocket, we put him on the bread hot, it melts nice … is gut! *(Coaxing.)* Please. Taste a bit for Rudy. If you don't like—phut! *(He mimes spitting on the floor.)* But you will like! Never have you tasted such bread as Rudy bakes. Bread of the angels. *(Holding the bread out to him.)* Please. One bite.

*(DANCOCK strikes the bread out of his hand. BRAUN picks it up, offers it again.)*

Please!

*(DANCOCK slaps it out of his hand again. BRAUN gazes at the bread on the floor; his shoulders begin to shake with soundless weeping.)*

I do not wish to be king of this place any more. It is too hard a place. Do not leave me. Take me with you.

DANCOCK: I can't take you with me.

BRAUN: *(Begging.)* You are my friend. Don't leave me here alone. You are strong. Rudy is weak. They do terrible things to the weak. *(He picks up the bread.)* Eat and stay strong. Eat.

DANCOCK: Don't ask me to eat your bread. I can't do it. *(Pause.)* I can't do it.

> *(As the lights go down, BRAUN clutches the bread to his chest, dismayed, as DANCOCK slowly, methodically, rips off the bandages.)*

### Scene Five

> *(Light suggesting a hospital late at night. KENNEALY enters drunk.)*

KENNEALY: By the suffering Jesus, didn't we black old Kaiser Bill's eyes for him but good and proper! Well, that's life for you. Lesson number one. Everybody's looking for a face to put a fist in. *(Remembering the Kaiser.)* And how the mighty are brought low! The Hun, down for the count! Down for the count as of eleven o'clock, the eleventh day of this cold and frosty fucking eleventh month. A knockout blow! Here's to us and piss on them! *(Drinks, turns maudlin.)* "In Flanders fields the poppies blow/ Between the crosses row on row," *(He can't remember the words, mumbles in cadence, recalls a few more lines.)* "If ye break faith with us who die/ We shall not sleep, though poppies grow/ In Flanders fields." *(Raises the flask in a toast.)* To the glorious dead!

> *(He hears a sound off stage and wheels about in alarm.)*

Who's there? *(Struggles to hide the flask in his pocket.)* Who's there? *(He waits. When no one answers he recovers his swaggering air.)* Thought it might be our very own Mr. Superintendent come creepy Christering about to check that all are dutiful at their posts. Like fucking Peeping Tom, looking in the window at the old scrub woman's tits. *(Laughs. Drinks. Speaks with a wistful, disappointed air.)* They'll be burning Kaiser Bill in effigy on Main Street about now. Firecrackers. Roman candles. Booze. A girl or two no better than she ought to be. Best night of the war. And me missing out because of old Holier Than Thou. "Can't spare staff with so many down with the flu," says his nibs. Leave Kennealy to find his cheer on the sly, like a rat in the corner, locked up with this lot. *(KENNEALY pauses, looks moodily around him.)* We mustn't lock the bastards in the wards, go skeleton staff for once, so some could enjoy an evening out. Oh no, out of the question! What if there was a fire! They wouldn't have a fighting chance, would they, locked up? *(Pause.)* Who gives a fuck? *(Pause.)* Nobody. End of discussion. *(Vehement.)* And if somebody was to drop a match, what would be the result? I'll tell you. One big sigh of thanksgiving and relief, one end of the province to the other. "Uncle Bertie, flamed in the Mental! What a shame! How many years was he there? Ten? Twenty you say! My, who'd have thought! *(Pause.)* But it's all for the best when you think of it. His suffering at an end." Our suffering at an end. *(Pause.)* Because I'll let you in on a dirty little secret. Their own flesh and blood don't want anything to do with them. And why? *(Shouts.) Because nobody in their right fucking mind would!* End of discussion. *Because nobody in their right fucking mind would!*

> *(KENNEALY whirls around at a sound off stage.)*

Sir? Superintendent?

> *(He listens. Another sound. KENNEALY edges nervously towards it, tucking the flask in his pocket.)*

Kennealy here, sir. Pay no mind to me. Only talking to myself to while away the lonesome hours of the night. *(Pause.)* No harm in anything said. *(Hesitating whether he should investigate further.)* Superintendent? *(Taking a deep breath.)* A word if you're there. *(Alarmed.)* Jumping Jesus!

> *(BRAUN, ghost-like in a long white nightgown, bursts across the stage. KENNEALY and he collide and BRAUN falls to the floor. KENNEALY, ready to flee, suddenly realizes who it is when BRAUN tries to scramble away on all fours. KENNEALY kicks him brutally.)*

German bastard! You damn near gave me a heart attack! What were you doing in that closet! Spying? You spying on me!

BRAUN: Stop! Please stop! I go to see my friend! I go to see Lieutenant Dancock! He needs Rudy! Let me go to my friend!

KENNEALY: *(Still kicking him.)* Go to the devil!

> *(BRAUN collapses under the assault. A sudden explosion of fireworks and cheering halts KENNEALY's attack.)*

Fireworks. Aren't they having a high old time in town tonight.

BRAUN: *(Crawling.)* I must go to my friend Lieutenant Dancock. My friend needs me. He needs Rudy's bread so he does not die.

KENNEALY: *(Taunting.)* He's a dead man, Fritz. Nothing you can do. Only a matter of time.

BRAUN: *(Trying to get to his feet.)* I don't listen to this! I go to my friend—

KENNEALY: Oh no, you don't! You aren't going anywhere!

*(KENNEALY puts his hand on BRAUN's head to shove him back to the floor, then snatches it back as if he had touched red hot metal.)*

Christ, you're burning up with fever!

BRAUN: I go to my friend. My friend wants me.

KENNEALY: *(Horrified.)* You bastard, you've got the flu. *(He wipes his hand on his smock. Backs away, rummaging in his pockets.)* My mask. Where's my mask?

BRAUN: *(Crawling aimlessly about the floor.)* Lieutenant Dancock. Lieutenant Dancock.

*(KENNEALY turns and flees.)*

*Lieutenant Dancock!*

### Scene Six

*(DANCOCK is in bed asleep. The SOLDIER sits on a chair near the bed, in shadows, keeping a death watch. BRAUN enters, scarcely able to walk.)*

BRAUN: Lieutenant. Lieutenant.

DANCOCK: *(Wakes, rises up in bed. In a rusty, hoarse voice.)* Rudy! What is it?

*(DANCOCK sees the SOLDIER and momentarily freezes. The SOLDIER doesn't move, only watches with detachment. DANCOCK climbs out of bed, but is so weak he has to support himself by leaning on it.)*

Rudy, you're hurt! What happened?

BRAUN: *(Explaining.)* He does this to me because I am weak.

DANCOCK: Who? Who does this to you?

BRAUN: Him. *(A reluctant pause.)* Mr. Kennealy.

DANCOCK: *(Shocked.)* Kennealy did this to you?

BRAUN: Kennealy. He does bad things to Rudy.

DANCOCK: Why? Why did he do this to you?

BRAUN: Because ... because I am afraid! Because I am weak! *(Pause. Pleading.)* If you go, I want to go too. Take me with you when you go.

*(With this announcement the SOLDIER rises from the chair and approaches BRAUN. BRAUN doesn't see him. The SOLDIER has found new prey.)*

DANCOCK: *(Desperately.)* Rudy, Rudy, listen to me! You mustn't say that! Not here! Not in front of—

SOLDIER: Let him decide for himself.

DANCOCK: Rudy, listen to me! You've got to listen to me!

BRAUN: Why! You never listen to Rudy! If you don't stay, then Rudy must find his own way out!

*(BRAUN looks around desperately, searching for a way out. The SOLDIER takes him by the elbow and begins to guide him from the room.)*

DANCOCK: Rudy! Rudy! Stop!

*(BRAUN halts. He and the SOLDIER turn toward DANCOCK.)*

*(Unwilling to promise.)* If you stay ... I will stay too.

BRAUN: Yes?

DANCOCK: You bring me some of your good bread, Rudy. I'll eat it. We'll eat it together. *(Pause.)* Until we're both strong.

*(BRAUN attempts to return to DANCOCK's bed. He collapses. The SOLDIER smiles contemptuously, shakes his head, and with a backward glance at DANCOCK, exits. )*

Help! Help! Somebody! Somebody please help us!

### Scene Seven

*(KENNEALY and the SUPERINTENDENT enter.)*

KENNEALY: We can't go on like this, Superintendent!

SUPERINTENDENT: We'll go on. We have no choice but to go on.

KENNEALY: We can't wedge one more cot into the infirmary. It's full to overflowing. This morning three more orderlies and four more nurses came down with the flu. Those of us who aren't sick are dead on our feet.

SUPERINTENDENT: Yes, yes. I know.

KENNEALY: Now two of the cooks are down. Last night nothing but bread and butter for supper. A man can't work on bread and butter.

SUPERINTENDENT: I'm working on bread and butter.

KENNEALY: There's not enough of us to do the job. We're losing control on the wards. Patients roaming the corridors. Screaming day and night. They smell the fear.

SUPERINTENDENT: We will not lose control of the wards as long as we do not lose control of ourselves. *(Pause.)* So let us get on with business. *(Pause.)* How many deaths reported yesterday?

KENNEALY: Eleven. And there'll be more today. *(Pause.)* The corpses are piling up. Nobody to bury them.

SUPERINTENDENT: It's November. Corpses will keep. We must concentrate on the living. I need you in the infirmary today. Come.

*(The SUPERINTENDENT moves off briskly. KENNEALY does not follow. The SUPERINTENDENT stops, turns around.)*

Are you deaf? I said I needed you in the infirmary.

KENNEALY: *(Stubbornly.)* No, sir.

SUPERINTENDENT: No, sir?

KENNEALY: You won't see my shadow darken that particular door. I won't do it.

SUPERINTENDENT: Come along, Mr. Kennealy. This instant. We're wasting time.

KENNEALY: I wasn't hired to nurse flu patients. I've got my rights.

SUPERINTENDENT: Rights? How dare you talk of rights when there are helpless people who depend on us!

KENNEALY: I'm not risking my skin in the infirmary.

SUPERINTENDENT: What you risk, Kennealy, is dismissal! That's what you bloody risk! Now do as you're told!

KENNEALY: Remember you once said if you and I were not of one mind I'd better get out. Well, we're not of one mind on this. *(Pause.)* So do I get out?

SUPERINTENDENT: What are you trying to pull?

KENNEALY: It's just that now the shoe's on the other foot. Now you need me more than I need you. It's like this. I'll work the wards and only the wards—or I'll go.

SUPERINTENDENT: This is monstrous!

KENNEALY: And if I go, you're short one more man to mind the lunatics. I don't think you can afford that. It's only logic.

SUPERINTENDENT: There's a point when logic becomes obscene, Kennealy.

KENNEALY: Well, I'm not a philosopher like yourself so I wouldn't know. *(Pause.)* So what's it going to be? Do I stay or do I go?

*(The SUPERINTENDENT cannot bring himself to speak.)*

Which?

SUPERINTENDENT: *(Defeated he says softly.)* Stay.

KENNEALY: Didn't catch that, sir.

SUPERINTENDENT: Stay!

KENNEALY: Very good, sir. Seeing as you ask so nicely.

*(KENNEALY begins to exit, pauses.)*

A word to the wise, sir. Don't push the staff too hard. This is a dangerous place. It wouldn't take much for them to walk.

*(KENNEALY exits. The SUPERINTENDENT, in despair, pulls up his mask and exits on the opposite side of the stage.)*

### Scene Eight

*(The infirmary. BRAUN is in bed, unconscious. DANCOCK is sponging his face.)*

DANCOCK: *(Emotional.)* I ate this morning. Half a loaf of bread, a quart of milk. Do you hear me, Rudy? I ate just as you asked me to, I ate to get strong. Strong enough to nurse you. Strong enough to—*(Breaks off at the thought.)* That's right. I'm eating for Kennealy, too. And when I'm strong again, one day Kennealy and I will meet face to face on one of those deserted staircases. Or when he takes me for a stroll in the grounds, we'll stop for a smoke behind one of those caragana hedges, out of the wind, and I'll ...

*(The SUPERINTENDENT enters.)*

SUPERINTENDENT: Dancock? *(Moves quickly towards him.)* Is that you, Dancock? *(Alarmed.)* What are you doing in the infirmary? Why didn't one of the nurses stop you? Nurse! Nurse!

DANCOCK: There are no nurses here. Only me.

SUPERINTENDENT: No nurses? Why are there no nurses—*(Breaking off in surprise.)* You spoke!

DANCOCK: I came to visit Rudy. He was burning with fever. I got a sponge and some water—

SUPERINTENDENT: Yes, yes, I see. But this is no place for you, Lieutenant. You're ill yourself. We must get you back to bed.

DANCOCK: I'm not going back to bed. Rudy needs me.

SUPERINTENDENT: Your friend is ill with the flu. Added to that Kennealy tells me he took a very bad tumble down the stairs. What he needs is expert nursing.

DANCOCK: They're sick themselves.

SUPERINTENDENT: Who?

DANCOCK: The nurses.

*(The SUPERINTENDENT is shaken by this news.)*

It's collapsing, Superintendent. Your whole house of cards is collapsing.

SUPERINTENDENT: The hell it is!

DANCOCK: No nurses. No proper food. Toilets overflowing. The dead left to lie in their beds.

SUPERINTENDENT: I won't let it collapse!

DANCOCK: What do you mean? One man can't hold this together.

SUPERINTENDENT: I have to. I'm all there is. *(Fiercely.)* The staff are ready to desert me. What am I to do?

DANCOCK: Ask for help.

SUPERINTENDENT: Good God! You think I haven't wired the Government for help? But it's the same everywhere. There's no help to spare.

DANCOCK: Then ask me.

SUPERINTENDENT: You? What do you mean?

DANCOCK: Is it so hard? Ask me.

SUPERINTENDENT: I don't see what you're saying.

DANCOCK: What if a man who refused to work in the past was to volunteer to empty bedpans, scrub floors, nurse the sick. What would that signal to the others? Patients like myself. Patients who are capable of grasping the danger we are in.

SUPERINTENDENT: No. Out of the question.

DANCOCK: Peel potatoes, bury the dead—

SUPERINTENDENT: I said no!

DANCOCK: What are you afraid of, Superintendent?

SUPERINTENDENT: Afraid of?

DANCOCK: Perhaps you are afraid that we will save ourselves when you could not.

*(The two men stare at each other. )*

SUPERINTENDENT: And if I were to ask your help in saving my hospital? What do you propose?

DANCOCK: Assemble the patients still on the wards. I will speak to them.

SUPERINTENDENT: You will speak to them?

DANCOCK: *(Definitely.)* I will speak to them.

SUPERINTENDENT: Very well then. You will speak to them.

### Scene Nine

*(DANCOCK walks to the edge of the stage with a clipboard in his hand. He addresses the audience as if they were inmates of the hospital.)*

DANCOCK: You are wondering why this meeting has been called. It has been called to ask you to work. To work to save all our lives. Orderlies, nurses, cooks, everyone we depended on—expect no more from them. They are sick, some are dead. *(Pause.)* I have a friend, a victim of the flu, who this morning I found ... who I found lying in his own vomit. With no one to clean him. I called for a nurse. There was none. I cleaned him. *(Pause.)* If we do not want to die like flies in a bottle, buzzing against the glass, then we must work. Not the kind of work they asked us to do before. Weaving willow baskets, tatting, crocheting, embroidering. We must do real work. Life and death work. *(Pause.)* Do not expect them to comfort the dying. Comfort them yourselves. Do not expect them to cook your soup. Cook it yourself. Cook it for the bedridden, the child with water on the brain, the senile old man, the epileptic. *(Pause.)* Do you understand me? I am asking for a cook. *(Pause.)* Can any of you cook? *(Surveys the audience, spots someone.)* Is your hand up or down? Up! State your credentials then. No need to be shy. *(Listens.)* Ten years a cook for CPR gangs. Good! The kitchen's yours! Soup and custard for the sick! *(Makes a mark on the clipboard.)* We need nursing volunteers.

*(Scans the audience. Indicates each volunteer by pointing.)* Yes. All right. Good. That's the spirit! We have four. Going once, going twice—Better! Five! Report to the Superintendent. He'll assign you your duties. Launderers. Dishwashers. Right you are, sir! Thank you, madam! *(Flicks pencil on paper for each.)* Grave digger. *(Pause.)* A grave digger, please. *(Long pause.)* They're stacking corpses like cordwood in an outhouse. *(Quietly.)* Thank you, sir. *(Makes his last mark on the sheet.)* Look lively then. To business. Dismissed.

> *(DANCOCK studies the sheet of paper on his clipboard. DOROTHEA enters. He catches sight of her.)*

Miss Gage!

DOROTHEA: How I missed our conversations, Mr. Dancock. Did you miss our conversations? *(Tentatively.)* You cannot imagine how distressed I was when I learned you were ... not well. I asked to visit you but the Superintendent said that was impossible. *(Pause.)* You are better now?

> *(DANCOCK nods, not sure whether he is or not.)*

*(With suppressed excitement.)* I stood there in the doorway, listening and watching. I have always found your conversation charming, but your oratory is inspiring! I would have joined the rest, but to volunteer in front of others ... *(Impulsively.)* I want to help, Mr. Dancock!

DANCOCK: *(Shaking his head.)* It is too dangerous.

DOROTHEA: I can strip beds, empty bedpans—

DANCOCK: No.

DOROTHEA: Fetch food and water, scrub floors—

DANCOCK: *(To dissuade her.)* And nurse the sick? Can you bring yourself to touch another human being?

DOROTHEA: I can wash the dead! If I catch fire I cannot harm the dead!

DANCOCK: But you can catch the flu.

DOROTHEA: *(Blazing up.)* You were very eloquent on the subject of crocheting and embroidering just now! And now you ask me to embroider! *(Pause. Continues more calmly.)* I hung on your words. Because, you see, all my life I have been an embroiderer. I embroidered in my father's house. I embroidered here. *(Pause.)* I want to do something besides embroider.

DANCOCK: My concern is for your safety—

DOROTHEA: Safety! Safety! *(Pause.)* Imagine a young woman sitting in the parlour of her father's house, counting stitches, counting the ticks of the clock, counting and counting and counting— *(Breaks off, resumes in a quieter, confessional vein.)* You don't think that is devilish hot work? Your head boils and seethes, you can scarcely catch your breath, you choke, you stifle with the heat. Do you have any idea how many times I came near to bursting into flames? That was danger! This, this is child's play!

DANCOCK: Hardly child's play!

DOROTHEA: I can weigh the risks as well as anyone who stood before you in this room.

> *(The look at each other, the question hanging in the balance.)*

> *(Quietly.)* You are not my Papa. I will have my freedom.

DANCOCK: Will you?

DOROTHEA: Yes, I will.

> *(DANCOCK, in spite of himself, smiles.)*

So it is settled. *(Pause.)* And it appears you are free too.

DANCOCK: Am I?

DOROTHEA: No more horrible Kennealy dogging your heels.

DANCOCK: *(Mood instantly darkening.)* No more horrible Kennealy.

DOROTHEA: What's wrong? What have I said?

DANCOCK: Rudy didn't fall down the stairs. Kennealy beat him.

DOROTHEA: Does the Superintendent know?

> *(DANCOCK shakes his head.)*

Then you must tell him!

DANCOCK: No. He would dismiss Kennealy and send him away. *(Ominously.)* I want Kennealy within reach. I'm going to make him pay for what he did.

DOROTHEA: Don't think such things! You are not a man who thinks such things!

DANCOCK: How do you know what I think? You know nothing about me.

DOROTHEA: I know you make me laugh. You invite me to dance.

DANCOCK: There is more to me than jokes and invitations.

DOROTHEA: There is more to all of us here than meets the eye. Haven't you learned that yet?

*(DANCOCK goes to a window, avoiding the topic.)*

DANCOCK: It's growing dark. Night comes early in November.

*(DOROTHEA joins him. They both peer out of the window. The SOLDIER enters, peers out over their shoulders.)*

DOROTHEA: The wind is coming up.

DANCOCK: A storm.

*(All stand motionless listening to the wind. The light alters to suggest the descent of darkness.)*

### Scene Ten

*(DOROTHEA is in the infirmary. BRAUN is in a bed. DANCOCK enters.)*

DANCOCK: *(Tearing off his mask.)* Christ! Four more dead.

DOROTHEA: Your mask!

DANCOCK: To hell with masks! What difference have they made.

*(DOROTHEA slowly pulls down hers.)*

Please don't do that. I spoke without thinking.

*(However, neither of them raises their masks.)*

DOROTHEA: Mr. Braun is finally asleep. We should sleep too. Morning comes soon enough.

DANCOCK: Rudy's worse. Fluid on the lungs. His breathing's very ragged.

DOROTHEA: You have to rest. You haven't slept in over forty-eight hours.

DANCOCK: In the trenches you learn to live without sleep.

DOROTHEA: You are killing yourself. You look terrible.

DANCOCK: Can a man be homesick for death? Miss it? It's all I knew for four years ... the smell of death. *(Pause.)* There was a man hanging in the wire, directly in front of our parapet, twenty yards off. We didn't know who he belonged to, he was caked in mud. No making out his uniform. You could smell him when the breeze was right. But that was no help. French, German, Canadian? *(Pause.)* Out there, in No Man's Land, at night the wounded used to cry for us to come out and save them. We didn't dare.

Flares opened in the black sky, turning everything bright as day. Like dying on a stage, I used to think, in the limelight, before an audience of thousands. *(Turning to the beds.)* They're still crying out to be saved. Listen.

DOROTHEA: You have to sleep. You are on the point of collapse.

DANCOCK: *(Anguished.)* How can I sleep?

DOROTHEA: *(Gently.)* Come with me. Let me put you to bed.

DANCOCK: I must stay.

DOROTHEA: But why?

DANCOCK: For Rudy. *(Exhausted and slightly confused.)* And there is someone else ...

DOROTHEA: Who?

DANCOCK: Someone. I'm expecting someone.

> *(DOROTHEA realizes she has no power over him.)*

DOROTHEA: I shall fetch the Superintendent. He will make you leave.

> *(DOROTHEA rushes out, leaving DANCOCK rooted to the spot, lost in what passes through his mind. The SOLDIER enters, pushing KENNEALY on a bed.)*

SOLDIER: Look who I brought to visit, Lieutenant. *(Beckons him.)* Come. Take a peek.

> *(DANCOCK stumbles to the bed, looks down at KENNEALY.)*

> *(Like a fond parent.)* Sleeping like a baby.

> *(DANCOCK stares.)*

You wanted him, didn't you? You have plans for him?

DANCOCK: *(With difficulty.)* Yes.

SOLDIER: Well, I'm delivering him. The bastard's all yours.

> *(They both gaze down at KENNEALY.)*

Helpless as a kitten. *(He walks over to BRAUN's bed.)* Braun too. Of course, he always was. If I were to put money on one of them living, I'd put it on Kennealy. Because bastards usually pull through, don't they, Lieutenant?

> *(DANCOCK doesn't answer.)*

What a shame though. For Rudy to die and Kennealy to get off scot free. *(Pause. Louder.)* If I remember correctly, you don't like that—people getting away with things.

*(DANCOCK says nothing.)*

Looks like it's in your hands again. To make sure somebody doesn't get away with something.

*(DANCOCK stares down at KENNEALY.)*

SOLDIER: The state he's in now—weak as a baby—you can do with him whatever you like.

DANCOCK: Yes.

SOLDIER: Would you like to?

*(DANCOCK doesn't answer.)*

Let me show you.

*(He drops to his knees, unbuckles DANCOCK's belt, slips it off, and demonstrates how to make a noose of it.)*

*(Demonstrating.)* See? *(He presses it into DANCOCK's hand.)* I think he should be awake. I think he should realize what's happening to him and why.

*(DANCOCK nods.)*

Wake him up.

*(DANCOCK, like an automaton, takes KENNEALY by the shoulder and gives him a half-hearted shake.)*

*(Excited.)* That's it! Wake him up! Wake him up!

*(DANCOCK shakes harder. The SOLDIER grows excited.)*

Make him pay! Make the bastard pay!

*(DANCOCK's shaking of KENNEALY becomes more and more frantic, reaching a crescendo. Suddenly he pushes himself away from KENNEALY, horrified at what he is doing.)*

DANCOCK: I can't!

SOLDIER: Can't? Can't?

DANCOCK: *(Whispering.)* No.

SOLDIER: Oh, isn't Lieutenant lovely? Isn't he sweet? Found a conscience, has he? So why not Kennealy? Why won't you do Kennealy? Why me and not this bag of shit!

DANCOCK: I had no choice with you.

SOLDIER: Liar.

DANCOCK: *(Defending himself.)* I had a responsibility to my men. To safeguard morale.

SOLDIER: Hypocrite. Self-righteous worm.

> *(DOROTHEA enters. Neither DANCOCK nor the SOLDIER are aware of her. She stops, stares, shrinks back into the shadows of a corner, a silent witness to what follows.)*

DANCOCK: How dare you call me names! You, a disgrace to the uniform! The worst kind of soldier. A barrack's thief! Malingerer! Defeatist!

SOLDIER: Coward, don't forget coward!

DANCOCK: Insolent!

SOLDIER: Insolent! Fancy that!

DANCOCK: Coward then! Filthy coward!

SOLDIER: *(Simply.)* Guilty as charged. *(Pause.)* And you?

> *(The two stand staring at each other.)*

DANCOCK: I knew you were ready to break. You showed all the signs. Not long before—*(Breaks off, suddenly remembering.)*

SOLDIER: You saw me dancing in a cafe. You've never forgotten that. How I looked.

DANCOCK: Happy.

SOLDIER: Yes. Happy. The last bit of fun before the big show.

DANCOCK: The big show, four hours of artillery to soften Gerry up. Orders to go over the top at 6:45. At 6:40 I told the platoon to stand to and fix bayonets.

SOLDIER: I let my rifle drop.

DANCOCK: I went down the line—

SOLDIER: —and shouted in my face—

DANCOCK: *(Shouting in his face.)* Pick up your weapon, Private! Pick it up!

SOLDIER: *(Small, frightened voice.)* No.

DANCOCK: No! Think again!

SOLDIER: *(As before.)* No.

DANCOCK: We officers had been warned. Of mutinies in the French army, in British labour battalions. Stamp out insubordination, we were told. Refusal of an order on the field of battle is an offence punishable by death. *(To the SOLDIER.)* Don't say I didn't warn you! You were warned!

SOLDIER: I was warned.

DANCOCK: You began to whimper. Like a pup.

SOLDIER: *(Whimpering.)* Jesus, Jesus, Jesus ...

DANCOCK: Don't give me any of your Jesus! There's no Jesus here and never has been! If you must pray to someone, pray to me, you yellow bastard! In this place, I'm the only Jesus there is. And Jesus says, Pick up your fucking rifle!

SOLDIER: I couldn't move.

DANCOCK: *(Correcting him.)* Wouldn't move. I took out my revolver.

SOLDIER: Put it to my head.

*(DANCOCK demonstrates.)*

DANCOCK: I was shaking like a leaf!

SOLDIER: I heard the hammer cock clear above the bombardment. How was it possible to hear the hammer cock?

DANCOCK: And still you wouldn't move!

SOLDIER: Couldn't! *(Pause.)* And you kept saying—

DANCOCK: Jesus is sitting in the judgement seat. And Jesus says you're going over the top. No more dodging, no more shirking. No more cheating your brothers in arms. No more asking them to wear your wounds and do your dying for you. Time to do your bit. Time to put your bloody shoulder to the wheel. Do as you're told or I'll send you to kiss the devil's arse! *(Wonder in his voice.)* And then you started to pray to me.

SOLDIER: Dear Jesus. Just this once. Don't make me do it. I can't do it. Please.

*(In the distance, the sound of whistles can be heard.)*

DANCOCK: Whistles started to blow. Attack whistles. Up and down the trenches. *(The sound of whistles grows louder, more insistent.)* I'd lost track of the time. Jesus late for the last trump. "Forward, boys! Forward!" I shouted. *(Pause. The memory is painful.)* Nobody moved. Up and down the line they were all going over the top but my boys didn't budge. *(Louder, shriller whistles, the sound of gunfire.)* I saw it in their eyes. If you were let off the hook—they weren't going either.

SOLDIER: The truth now!

DANCOCK: *(Desperate, urging on his men.)* Come on, boys! Forward!

SOLDIER: They aren't fools! They don't want to die either!

DANCOCK: *(Pleading.)* For the love of God, men! Advance!

SOLDIER: *(Cutting.)* God? For the love of Dancock, you mean!

> *(DANCOCK turns on him, enraged. Ear splitting whistles. Then a sudden silence. DANCOCK begins to speak with a terrible, pitiless determination.)*

DANCOCK: Pick up your rifle. You think I won't do it? I'll do it. *(Pause. Whistles resume.)* Pick it up! Pick it up! Pick it—

> *(The terrific report of a pistol. Silence.)*

*(Looking at his hands.)* There was blood on my hand. A gush of blood—*(He begins scraping at his hand with his nails.)* It was an accident ... An accident. *(To the audience.)* It was an accident!

SOLDIER: Liar.

DANCOCK: I did it for the men. They should have thanked me. They might have gone forward out of ... *(Blurts it.)* out of regard for me! But when I looked in their faces ...

SOLDIER: Yes. What did you see?

DANCOCK: That day marching to the boats ... There's nothing I wouldn't have done for my men. I would have died for them!

SOLDIER: *(Quietly.)* Fuck you. I died for them.

DANCOCK: You, you selfish bastard? You never died for anyone!

SOLDIER: Didn't I? Someone had to pay when your men turned on you. Face it, Dancock, they didn't love you, they despised you. And you despised them huddling there, shit-scared, all those white faces saying enough is enough. We aren't marching to the harbour, sir. We aren't in some schoolboy dream of glory, some Boy's Own fucking Annual! This is death. And we don't want any part of it. Not for you, not for anybody.

DANCOCK: It wasn't like that! It wasn't like that! You're twisting it—

SOLDIER: You betrayed yourself, Dancock. Your men had nothing to betray. *(Pause.)* Because love is only possible between equals.

*(DANCOCK stares at him.)*

And now, finally, we are equals.

DANCOCK: The hell we are! You, a dirty little liar, a common thief, a coward—

SOLDIER: *(Interrupting.)* And you a murderer.

DANCOCK: What do you want with me!

SOLDIER: I couldn't say no to you and live. You can't say no to me and live. There's no denying me, Dancock, or what you did. *(Pause.)* Look me in the face.

DANCOCK: No!

SOLDIER: Look me in the face.

DANCOCK: No!

SOLDIER: Look at me!

*(Slowly, DANCOCK looks up at him.)*

Remember? You promised to send me to kiss the devil's arse. And you did. Now you must kiss it too.

DANCOCK: What do you mean?

SOLDIER: *(Puckers lewdly.)* Kiss the devil's arse, Dancock.

DANCOCK: No!

SOLDIER: Kiss me!

*(DANCOCK approaches, drawn against his will.)*

*(With a commanding gesture.)* Kiss me!

*(DANCOCK reluctantly kisses him on the cheek. The SOLDIER grips him and passionately kisses his mouth. DANCOCK is overcome with revulsion and shock.)*

The taste of what you did. Think of it as your souvenir of France. If you happen to lose that taste—you can expect me back. Goodnight, Lieutenant.

*(The SOLDIER salutes, exits. DOROTHEA moves to comfort DANCOCK.)*

DOROTHEA: It's all right. He's gone.

DANCOCK: *(In disbelief.)* You were here? You saw him?

DOROTHEA: Of course.

DANCOCK: You heard?

*(DOROTHEA nods.)*

How can that be?

DOROTHEA: Why shouldn't I see what you see? After all we've been through together?

DANCOCK: But ...

DOROTHEA: You saw my phoenix, didn't you?

DANCOCK: *(Ashamed.)* Yes. But what you've just seen of me ... that's different.

DOROTHEA: It doesn't matter.

DANCOCK: But it has to matter!

DOROTHEA: Darkness and fire! That's what we've seen and what matters!

DANCOCK: Darkness and fire?

DOROTHEA: The dead. The phoenix. We've seen them both now! Haven't we? *(She moves to Braun's bed.)* Mr. Braun's breathing is easier. Come, listen!

*(DANCOCK gets to his feet and goes to the bed. DOROTHEA has already moved to Kennealy's bed. She takes a mirror out of her pocket and holds it to his nostrils. Checks it. Slowly draws the sheet up over his face. DANCOCK turns and sees this.)*

*(Flatly.)* Kennealy is dead.

### Scene Eleven

*(DANCOCK sits on a chair in the ward. The SUPERINTENDENT enters.)*

SUPERINTENDENT: May I?

*(DANCOCK nods. The SUPERINTENDENT takes a chair.)*

Good news. No new cases today. Maybe it's the light at the end of the tunnel. And Braun is much improved. His lungs have cleared. He ate.

DANCOCK: *(Fondly.)* Dear Rudy. I'm glad.

SUPERINTENDENT: Out of 850 inmates, 500 cases of flu. 58 patients and 5 staff dead. *(Pause.)* It could have been much worse. If not for you—and the other volunteers. You saved this hospital.

*(DANCOCK looks away.)*

I did not see you at work in the infirmary today, Lieutenant Dancock.

DANCOCK: No.

SUPERINTENDENT: You're not feeling ill, are you?

DANCOCK: I could not face Miss Gage.

SUPERINTENDENT: Why?

DANCOCK: Because I am ashamed. Of something I did.

SUPERINTENDENT: So am I. *(The two men exchange a look of understanding, rapprochement.)* We cannot control everything can we? My mistake was to think I could. Remember me saying that I had kept this hospital an island from war and rumours of war? Well, no one can set a boundary to war. Our soldiers brought it home with them in their lungs and in their blood. The four horsemen ride where they will. *(Pause.)* I want you to know this. Whatever I did, I did because I believed it was necessary. This does not excuse it. But it may explain it.

DANCOCK: For some things there are explanations. Explanations can be lived with.

SUPERINTENDENT: Meaning?

DANCOCK: Whatever you did ... *(Starts again.)* I could live with your mistakes. *(Pause.)* I need a cigarette.

> *(The SUPERINTENDENT takes out his cigarette case and offers him one.)*

Of course, smoking on the ward is forbidden.

SUPERINTENDENT: True. But the exception proves the rule. *(Pause.)* You taught me the importance of exceptions. For that I'm grateful.

DANCOCK: *(Holding up the cigarette.)* And I ... I'm grateful for this.

### Scene Twelve

*(The set is arranged for a dance as it was in Act One. A murmur of excited conversation can be heard. The SUPERINTENDENT stands near a table supporting a gramophone, a punch bowl, a plate of sandwiches. DANCOCK and BRAUN are seated beside*

*each other. Across the room from them sits DOROTHEA in her blue dress. DANCOCK avoids meeting her gaze.)*

SUPERINTENDENT: *(Clapping his hands to attract their attention.)* Ladies and gentlemen! Ladies and gentlemen! Your attention, please! *(The room quietens.)* We are gathered here to reinstate an innocent pleasure of the past—our afternoon tea dances. *(Pause.)* There are some who thought this was not proper—that dancing should not tread so hard upon the heels of grief and death. *(Pause.)* I'm not so sure. *(Pause.)* I propose we dance.

> *(The SUPERINTENDENT starts the gramophone. All the characters appear to watch dancers on the floor. The SUPERINTENDENT casts anxious glances at DANCOCK. DOROTHEA waits hopefully for DANCOCK's invitation to dance. He remains in his chair while BRAUN urges him to take the floor.)*

BRAUN: The Lieutenant does not dance?

DANCOCK: No. He doesn't.

BRAUN: *(Indicating DOROTHEA.)* Maybe she likes you to dance.

DANCOCK: I am not fit to dance with Miss Gage.

BRAUN: *(Mistaking his meaning.)* What do you mean, not fit? You are the healthiest man here. If you are not fit—Rudy is not fit. Because Rudy lay on death's door mat for how long?

DANCOCK: A long time.

BRAUN: But my loyal subjects cry, "God save the King! Long live the King!" And what happens? *(Ecstatic.)* I rise! I rise!

DANCOCK: *(With a knowing, sad smile.)* Indeed you do, Rudy.

BRAUN: *(Shaking his finger at DANCOCK.)* You were not sick and yet you make the excuse you are not fit. Rudy was sick as a dog and already he wants to dance all day and all night. The sick dog's tail wants to wiggle and wag! *(Pause.)* You think Matron would like a wiggle of the old dog's tail? Ja?

DANCOCK: I think the sick dog better eat a sandwich to keep his strength up. Go and get yourself a sandwich, Rudy.

BRAUN: Ja. The English cucumber sandwich. Water and air.

> *(BRAUN goes to get himself a sandwich. He and the SUPERIN-TENDENT stand commenting on the imagined dancers.*

*DOROTHEA casts discreetly encouraging looks DANCOCK's way. He cannot bring himself to look at her. At last DOROTHEA rises and strides across the floor to him.)*

DOROTHEA: *(Decisively.)* May I have the honour of this dance, Mr. Dancock?

*(The record ends. Everybody's attention is focused on them.)*

DANCOCK: Miss Gage ... I—

DOROTHEA: Has no one ever invited you to dance before?

*(DANCOCK looks at her, struck by the phrase. He still hesitates.)*

Please. If only because I ask you.

DANCOCK: I can't see why you would. Knowing what you know.

DOROTHEA: *(Gently.)* I am asking you to dance with me, John.

*(DANCOCK gets to his feet, fumbles to pull on his gloves.)*

No gloves. A lady does not dance with a gentleman wearing gloves such as those. *(Tenderly.)* This is my coming out. My first dance. I wish things to be done correctly.

*(DANCOCK gets hurriedly to his feet, lays his gloves on the chair.)*

DOROTHEA: Of course, I put you in terrible danger by touching you. If I should ignite.

DANCOCK: My dear Miss Gage—

DOROTHEA: *(Correcting him.)* Dorothea.

DANCOCK: *(Gravely gallant.)* My dear Dorothea. Not so very long ago I tried to dissuade you from becoming a nurse. I was told then that I should leave you to weigh the risks for yourself. *(Pause.)* What is true of you is also true of me.

*(DOROTHEA smiles, takes him by the hand, leads him on to the dance floor.)*

DOROTHEA: And if we burst into flames—what of it?

*(DOROTHEA and DANCOCK come together to dance. They dance for a brief time with a grave and dignified joy, immersed in each other and the music. Blackout.)*